JUNIA

JUNIA
THE FIRST WOMAN APOSTLE

ELDON JAY EPP

Foreword by Beverly Roberts Gaventa

FORTRESS PRESS
MINNEAPOLIS

Cover image: Empress Theodora and attendants. Mosaic from the south wall of the apse, S. Vitale, Ravenna, Italy, c. 547 C.E. Photo copyright © Cameraphoto Arte, Venice/Art Resource, N.Y. Used by permission.
Cover design: Laurie Ingram

Library of Congress Cataloging-in-Publication Data
Epp, Eldon Jay.
 Junia : the first woman apostle / Eldon Jay Epp ; foreword by Beverly Roberts Gaventa.
    p. cm.
 Includes bibliographical references and index.
 ISBN 0-8006-3771-2 (alk. paper)
 1. Junia (Biblical figure) 2. Bible. N.T. Romans XVI, 7—Criticism, interpretation, etc. I. Title.
 BS2460.J88E66 2005
 227'.1092—dc22
                                    2005020402

The paper used in this publication meets the minimum requirements of American National Standard for Information Sciences—Permanence of Paper for Printed Library Materials, ANSI Z329.48-1984.

Manufactured in the U.S.A.
09   08   07   06   05   1   2   3   4   5   6   7   8   9   10

This book is dedicated, with affection, to my grandsons,

NATHANIEL GREGORY MERRELL
and
ANDREW JAMES MERRELL

May they live in a more egalitarian world.

CONTENTS

FOREWORD

THE GREETINGS OF Romans 16 are easy to skip. With a few exceptions, the names themselves are unfamiliar to us. Although we know people named James, John, and Mary, we do not routinely encounter children named for Ampliatus, Tryphosa, or Phlegon. Neither do the greetings themselves generate a lot of interest, with their formulaic expressions such as "Greet Prisca and Aquila," and "my beloved Stachys." Like the enumeration of Esau's descendants in Genesis 36 or the census lists of Numbers, it seems a safe assertion that the greetings of Romans 16 are read somewhat quickly, if at all. Impatience with Romans 16 manifests itself in my Romans class as often as the assignment rolls around. To be sure, it does not help that Romans 16 customarily falls at the end of the semester, when everyone involved is due for a rest from following the tortures of Paul's reasoning.

For many years, scholarly work on Romans contributed to the dispatch with which this passage was treated. The conventional wisdom that Romans was a summary of Christian theology caused attention to fall heavily on the doctrine unpacked in the letter, with little attention left over for the people the letter addressed. To make matters worse, many scholars regarded Romans 16 as a fragment of another letter, one never intended for believers at Rome. Taking these factors together with the sheer difficulty of following Paul's logic through the first fifteen chapters, it is easy to understand a certain indifference to Romans 16.

The last several decades have witnessed a marked change in the scholarly situation, however. To begin with, most scholars now agree that Romans, in common with other early Christian texts, was written in a specific context and to address a specific set of issues or concerns. Lively debate persists over what situation(s) produced this particular letter, but considerable agreement has developed that Romans is something other than a theological compendium.[1] In addition, text-critical and literary studies have produced a near consensus that Romans 16 is part of the original letter Phoebe delivered to Rome.[2] Perhaps most important, Peter Lampe's work on the first two centuries of Christianity at Rome has invigorated interest in the information that can be gleaned from the names of those mentioned in Romans 16.[3]

That combination of factors causes the eye to linger over Romans 16. Feminist scholars have paid particular attention to the names of women and what those names suggest about leadership in early Christianity and Paul's attitudes toward women in leadership. To begin with, he commends the deacon and benefactor, Phoebe, presumably because she delivers the letter and becomes its first interpreter as she reads it to believers gathered in scattered house churches. The greetings proper open in v. 3 with the names of the married couple Prisca and Aquila, both of whom are identified as Paul's fellow-workers. Included in list that follows are Mary, Tryphaena, Tryphosa, Persis, the mother of Rufus, Julia, and the sister of Nereus. Most important, several of these women are singled out for their labor on behalf of the gospel.

Paul also greets another woman, Junia, whose case Eldon Epp treats in this slender and important volume. Several studies have attended to Junia before,[4] but no one has addressed as many facets of the problem as Epp does. There are several issues that run through Epp's account, but two dominate. The first and most important issue concerns the name Junia and its presence during the two millennia since Phoebe first delivered the letter to Rome. Stated much too simply, the problem is as follows: in Romans 16:7, Paul greets a pair of people he identifies as "prominent among the apostles." The first is named Andronicus, a male name. And the second is named either Junia (feminine) or Junias/Junianus (masculine). The difference in Greek is a matter solely of the accentuation: one form of accent would indicate a feminine name and the other a masculine name.

The points Epp brings forward and develops are quite clear: For the first seven centuries of the church's life Greek manuscripts did not employ accents, but when accents did become common practice in the manuscript tradition, and insofar as those accents can be identified, they uniformly identify the name as feminine. To put the point sharply: there is no Greek manuscript extant that unambiguously identifies Andronicus's partner as a male. That consistent pattern coheres with the evidence offered by early Christian writers for the first thousand years of the church's life and well into the second thousand years. Theologians as diverse as Origen, Ambrosiaster, John Chrysostom, Jerome, Theodoret, John Damascene, Peter Abelard, and Peter Lombard, assume that the partner of Andronicus is a woman by the name of Junia. Particularly impressive is Chrysostom's observation concerning Junia: "How great the wisdom of this woman must have been that she was even deemed worthy of the title of apostle."[5] Only with the thirteenth century Aegidius of Rome, and especially with Martin Luther's translation, did the view arise that Junia was in fact a male, Junias. Finally, and not of least importance, the female name Junia is a widely attested Roman name, but there exists no evidence for the use of the masculine forms Junias or Junianus.

The second issue arises directly from the first: Since the case for the name Junia is so strong, how did a male replacement slip into her spot in Romans 16? Something happened during the first quarter of the twentieth century. As Epp thoroughly documents, prior to that time, critical editions of the Greek New Testament as well as English translations, with rare exceptions, identify Andronicus's partner as Junia and offer no alternate reading that would suggest there is any problem or ambiguity. Beginning with the thirteenth edition of the Nestle text in 1927, and somewhat earlier with English translations, the female Junia becomes the male Junias, So things remain until the 1970s, when once again Junia enters the picture. Even now, however, the NRSV offers "Junias" in the footnotes, and the NIV presents "Junias" with no further comment, leaving Andronicus with a male partner for whom there is no ancient evidence whatsoever.

One sobering lesson to take from the story Epp recounts concerns the way in which scholars do their work. Epp makes it painfully, maddeningly clear that a major factor in twentieth-century treatments of Romans 16:7 was the assumption that a woman could not have been an apostle. As the matter was somewhat delicately stated in the influential handbook of Hans Lietzmann, first published in 1906, the individual referred to must be a man "because of the following statements" identifying that person as an apostle.[6] That our sociocultural assumptions shape our exegetical interpretations is scarcely a new insight, but Epp's volume also reveals the sheer weight of scholarly tradition and the perils of work that is not sufficiently independent and critical. On page after page, we read of lexical entries that influence the choices made in critical editions of the Greek New Testament. Those critical editions in turn produce commentaries and monographs and contemporary translations. The result is not a little embarrassing to those charged with the scholarly investigation of biblical texts, and it should be greatly concerning to those who depend on those texts. In this particular case, what was nothing more than a house of cards had become an "assured" result of scholarship.

Of great import for many readers of Eldon Epp's book will be the fact that the greetings of Romans 16 contain one more woman's name than those of us educated in the twentieth century were led to believe. Her name is Junia, and Paul applies to her and her partner, Andronicus, the name "apostle." For the students in my classes who have read an earlier version of Epp's argument, the reaction is amazement. Readers of this book will soon join in their amazement.

For those Christians whose concern about women in leadership roles is tied to the question whether women actually served as leaders during the church's earliest generations, this book is an eye-opener. Whatever Paul may have intended with the tortured lines of 1 Corinthians 11:2-16, and whether or not he actually wrote 1 Corinthians 14:34-35, here the evidence of women taking active roles in leadership appears straightforward. According to Acts 2, Peter employs words of Joel at Pentecost to declare the fulfillment of God's promises, promises that include both "sons and daughters." The time has come to acknowledge the full participation of daughters alongside of sons in Romans 16 as well.

We are indebted to Eldon Epp. More than that, we are indebted to Junia, along with Phoebe, Prisca, Mary, and a host of women whose names we may never have, for their labors in building the church.

—Beverly Roberts Gaventa
Helen H. P. Manson Professor of
New Testament Literature and Exegesis
Princeton Theological Seminary

PREFACE

THIS BRIEF VOLUME has a short history. Some three years ago I was invited to contribute an essay to a volume honoring a colleague and friend, Professor Joël Delobel, upon his retirement from long service in the Department of Biblical Studies of the Faculty of Theology at the University of Leuven (Belgium). The article was published as "Text-Critical, Exegetical, and Socio-Cultural Factors Affecting the Junia/Junias Variation in Romans 16,7" in *Textual Criticism and Exegesis: Festschrift J. Delobel*, BETL 161, ed. A. Denaux (Leuven: Leuven University Press and Peeters, 2002), 227–91.

The author gratefully acknowledges the permission granted by Peeters Publishers, Leuven, to use the substance of the article in the present volume.

Professor Delobel, an accomplished New Testament exegete and textual critic, has written or edited more than one hundred publications, and through them he has demonstrated personally the motto for which he is well known: textual criticism and exegesis are "Siamese twins." Should anyone think that textual criticism functions mechanically and in isolation from the immediate and larger contexts of a given textual variation, nothing could be further from the truth. Accordingly, the long-standing reading of "Junias" in Romans 16:7 must be understood within the broad contexts of New Testament Greek grammar and usage, but particularly in the socio-cultural-theological contexts of European, British, and North American Christian scholarship during the past century. That is the burden of this book—to explain the basis in modern times on which Junia, a fellow worker with Paul, was denied her rightful place as an apostle, for she was in truth the first woman to be called "apostle."

The research for this volume was carried out primarily at Andover-Harvard Theological Library at the Harvard Divinity

School, and the original work was completed and published while the author was Visiting Lecturer (2001–2002) and Visiting Professor of New Testament (2002–2003 and 2004–2005) at the Divinity School. I am most grateful for the cordiality offered to me by Harvard professors François Bovon, Helmut Koester, Karen L. King, Elisabeth Schüssler Fiorenza, Laura Nasrallah, and former faculty members Ellen Bradshaw Aitken and Allen Callahan. I appreciate also the use of resources in other Harvard libraries and in those of the Episcopal Divinity School/Weston Jesuit School of Theology (Cambridge) and the Andover Newton Theological School (Newton Centre, Massachusetts).

I received invitations to present two lectures on Junia, first at the New Testament Colloquium of the Boston Theological Institute (November 2000) and later a public lecture at Wellesley College (March 2004) entitled "Junia: Apostle Deposed by Gender Change."

I welcome the appropriate foreword by Beverly Roberts Gaventa that graces this volume. It captures both the larger context as well as the immediate problems of Romans 16:7 as that passage has been transmitted to us in the Greek New Testament and in translations since the invention of printing. She and I were members of the 1987 Search Committee to secure the Society of Biblical Literature's first permanent Executive Director, and, in recent years, we served as members of the SBL Council, when she was Chair of Council and I was SBL Vice President and President (2002–2003). Earlier we were fellow members of a small Board that created the *Critical Review of Books in Religion*, of which she was the first and founding editor (1988–1990) and I was the second (1991–1994). Originally sponsored by the American Academy of Religion and SBL, eventually it became SBL's *Review of Biblical Literature*. Our paths have crossed also in other scholarly projects, and it is gratifying for me to have the endorsement of a theological seminary professor with close ecclesiastical ties to the church at large.

I am pleased that the Reverend Scott Tunseth, General Manager, Book Publishing Team, and J. Michael West, Editor-in-Chief of Fortress Press, afforded me the opportunity to make this study available to a wider audience in a revised and updated version. I am particularly grateful that they asked Dr. Marshall D. Johnson to shepherd the book through the publishing process; he and I shared the pleasure of working on the Hermeneia commentary series when he served as Director of Publishing for Fortress Press from 1990 to 1997 and I as secretary and member of the New Testament Editorial Board. Without his encouragement, competent assistance, and timely labors, the present volume would have been unduly delayed. I also thank Rebecca Lowe, who skillfully handled the volume's production with care and meticulous attention to detail.

Finally, I wish to report that early in the writing process the spell checker on my computer presaged my conclusion when it suggested that *Junias* should be replaced by *Junia*. But there were other suggestions as well, namely, that *Junia* should be read as *Julia*, reproducing the only actual variant to *Junia* in the Greek and versional manuscript tradition; that *Junia* should be replaced by *Junias* (a retrograde move!); and, most telling of all, that *Junias* should be corrected to *Judas*!

For me—and those like-minded—the task that lies ahead is to make only one of these corrections, and to make it stick: *Junias* must be corrected to *Junia*. I trust that both theoretically and actually the Apostle *Junias*, who had deprived *Junia* of a century of apostleship, has evaporated—and rightly so—for he was merely the figment of the wishful imagination of some influential white European, British, and American male scholars, caught up in but actively abetting a culturally shaped bias that wished to exclude women from leadership positions in the church—in this case a role that a named woman filled in the earliest period and fulfilled as an outstanding member.

PART I

CONTEMPORARY TEXTUAL CRITICISM

TEXTUAL CRITICISM
AND EXEGESIS

NEW TESTAMENT TEXTUAL critics for centuries have had an obsession to find the "Holy Grail," though in this case the quest has been for the "original text." But, like the Holy Grail, the "original" text is elusive and cannot be found, and she or he who claims to have found it will be unable to demonstrate with any measure of assurance that it has been found.[1] So, as textual critics, we do what we can: most of us have adjusted our goal to the recovery of the *earliest attainable text*, and—because the New Testament was so heavily copied and recopied prior to the invention of printing—the 5,600 Greek manuscripts contain such extensive mixture that an overall stemma or family tree cannot be reconstructed. So we have to work with each separate *variation-unit*—each separate set of variant readings at any given point in the text—and we attempt to recover the earliest attainable text by identifying, for example, the variant in each instance that best explains the rise of all the others. The result, to be found in the standard Nestle-Aland and the United Bible Societies' Greek New Testaments[2]—which all of us use and are delighted to have—is a constructed, average, and compromise text that does not exist, and probably never did exist, in any actual manuscript. The enormity of the task will be obvious from merely mentioning that there are perhaps a third of a million variant readings among the extant manuscripts of this rather small collection of writings we call the New Testament.

By nature, then, textual critics wallow in details, such as alternate readings consisting of a letter, a word, or a phrase; or varying spelling or word order; or the lack of one or several words at a point in the text. But they have to worry also about such minutiae not only in *Greek* manuscripts but in some

10,000 manuscripts in Syriac, Coptic, Latin, and a half dozen other ancient languages. If that were not enough, they must cope with variants in myriad citations of the New Testament scattered widely among early church writers. In short, the textual critic is always at risk of drowning in a sea of data and details. And there are other risks as well: In 1941, the prestigious *Proceedings of the British Academy* reported, following the publication of two volumes of meticulous textual apparatus for the Gospels of Mark and Matthew, that the eyes of Mr. Legg, the editor, "have given way under the strain."[3]

Whether it was the challenge of analyzing and classifying all these data, or perhaps in spite of the them, I found the subject fascinating many years ago. Soon, however, I moved on from such restricted and traditional tasks to pursue some of the larger issues raised by this array of textual variation. After all, textual criticism has its captivating detective side, inviting theories on the history and methods of the discipline and explanations for sizable groups of variants and for closely related manuscripts— all the while looking for what they might tell us about diverse aspects of early Christianity. I tackled first the complex problem of the so-called Western text of the book of Acts—a text whose numerous variants make Acts about 8 percent longer than its rival text—and my claim was that this longer text harbored an anti-Judaic bias.[4] These numerous variant readings had a story to tell—a rather distasteful one in this instance. Further explorations attempted to discover and to describe the intellectual and sociocultural context of our early New Testament papyrus manuscripts so as to illuminate their real-life environment, with special attention to the vast number of manuscripts found in Egypt at Oxyrhynchus.[5] Most recently I addressed the vexing problem of the multivalence of the term "original text."[6]

All of these endeavors are aspects of the current approach to New Testament textual criticism—the search for the earliest attainable text, the isolation of ideological tendency or bias in textual variants to expose the stories they have to tell, and the attempt to place manuscripts in their sociocultural and intellectual contexts. However, when the goal of New Testament textual criticism consisted of the restoration of a single original text, the significance of textual criticism for exegesis could also be described rather simplistically: Reconstruct the pristine text of the New Testament, or of its individual books and pericopes, and interpreters will know assuredly the exact text to be exegeted. More recently, however, both this simplicity and the accompanying innocence of New Testament textual criticism began to erode,[7] creating new obstacles for both textual critics and exegetes but also opening paths to new insights and opportunities.

This process of change had its precedents during the past two centuries of the discipline's history and development. For example, at the end of the nineteenth century, when it appeared to many—at least momentarily—that B. F. Westcott and F. J. A. Hort, in their so-called Neutral text type, had isolated *The New Testament in the Original Greek*,[8] it quickly became apparent that this "Neutral" text was neither as neutral nor as original as they had claimed. This was obvious enough merely from the ensuing discussion by various scholars of Westcott-Hort's so-called Western text type. After all, this "Western" (or, better, D-text) was held by them to be as early as (or perhaps earlier than) the "Neutral" (or, better, the B-text), yet Westcott-Hort had rejected the D-text as the "original" text because they viewed it as having been corrupted in the process of transmission.

Before Westcott-Hort there was Constantin Tischendorf, and before him Karl Lachmann, who (in 1831) made the decisive break with the *textus receptus* (the "text received" by all), which had been presumed since the sixteenth century to be the original form. Yet these are only a few figures in the well-known history of the quest for the "original text," a long story of the increasing and on-going uncertainty about what should be considered the most likely "original" or the earliest attainable New Testament text. This is not the place to repeat this extensive narrative. It is essential only to point out that, at least in this writer's judgment, textual critics must now speak of multivalence in the term "original text" and in many instances must be willing to confront both ambiguity and inevitable difficulty (if not frustration) when trying to determine the earlier or earliest reading in a given variation unit—and more so when dealing with the text of a whole writing or of the entire New Testament.[9] Indeed, in many variation units where meaningful variants are involved (and where scribal errors are not the obvious explanation), the search for a *single* original text or reading may have to be abandoned.[10] As a consequence, the exegete who pays more attention to textual criticism than merely consulting the currently dominant critical edition (Nestle–Aland[27] = UBS[4]) is now in a difficult situation, for such an exegete will, again and again, face hard decisions about which text or readings to exegete, or whether to exegete two or more readings as viable options for the dimensions of meaning a given text had in the early church or as options at various levels in the composition, transmission, and authority of a writing or a corpus in early Christianity. To take a simple kind of example, whether the textual variants "in Rome" (in Rom 1:7, 15) or "in Ephesus" (in Eph 1:1) have come into those writings at a later interpretive or perhaps canonical stage[11] affects not only (a) the interpretation of the sentences containing these phrases but also (b) issues of "introduction," such as the destination of these letters and indeed their very nature, and, more widely, (c) the collection of the Pauline corpus and its canonization.

Suddenly, then, it becomes obvious that to ask the apparently simple question about which text or reading to exegete whenever the New Testament shows meaningful textual variation, actually involves raising several concomitant (and more vexing) questions. Should we interpret a predecessor (and therefore a "more original") text-form that lies behind our canonical text-form (e.g., Romans with or without "in Rome" or a short, fourteen-chapter version of Romans, as revealed by the doxology found in a number of manuscripts after 14:23)? Or should we exegete an interpretive (and therefore a derivative) text-form that is now our canonical text but one that has been developed further, e.g., by heretical or orthodox rewritings of an established text?[12] Or should we exegete as the author's text of Acts the B-text or the approximately 8 percent longer D-text, or both (on the view that two versions were produced by a single author)?[13] Examples, of course, could be multiplied a hundredfold both from the larger and smaller cases of meaningful textual variation, ranging from large segments of text, such as the endings of Mark and the *pericope adulterae* (John 7:53—8:11), to variants of a word or two, such as the presence/absence of υἱοῦ θεοῦ (Son of God) in Mark 1:1 or the number of the beast in Rev 13:18 (which, incidentally, reads 666 in virtually all manuscripts, but 616 in C, a few other manuscripts, and now in one of the latest New Testament papyri to be published, 𝔓115).[14]

Considering the last two examples, an exegete is likely to spend little time on the variation unit in the Apocalypse because of the overwhelming attestation of the traditional number, but doubtless will expend considerable effort on the variant referred to in Mark 1:1 because of the far-reaching implications that flow from the choice made. The opening line of Mark is usually given as, "The beginning of the gospel of Jesus Christ, the Son of God" (RSV; cf. NRSV), which veils a rather evenly divided textual tradition of these two divine titles—"Christ" and "Son of God." Codex Sinaiticus (ℵ) and others, on one hand, have the full phrase, "Jesus Christ, Son of God," while Codices Vaticanus (B), Bezae (D), and Washingtonianus (W), with other witnesses, have only "Jesus Christ." An exegete who attempts a decision based solely on the manuscript attestation (external evidence) will face the unsettling fact that the two manuscripts generally deemed "best," namely, ℵ and B, go separate ways in this case. With closely divided manuscript evidence, however, a textual critic would move immediately to internal evidence (evidence from the transcriptional process—how scribes worked—and from the immediate and larger context of the variation unit). In this case, a rudimentary assessment of transcriptional evidence would support the shorter reading,[15] "Jesus Christ" without "Son of God," because Christian scribes, when encountering divine names, would be more likely to add the familiar, commonly associated words "Son of God" (as well as "Lord") to an existing "Jesus Christ" than to remove the former phrase if it were present in the exemplar. But the larger issue is the passage's context— here consisting perhaps of the Gospel of Mark *as a whole*! That is, do the words "Son of God" likely represent what the author wrote because Jesus as "Son of God" or Jesus' sonship is a major or crucial theme of this Gospel? If so, to exclude it by appealing to various other text-critical criteria might be to eradicate from the opening sentence the author's not-so-subtle declaration of a major theme for the entire work that follows. Naturally, whether "Son of God" serves Mark's Gospel in this way is a question for exegetes to answer, and indeed they have answered it both positively and negatively, but a point to be noted is that not only does textual criticism affect exegesis, but exegesis affects textual criticism in case after case.

This important interaction between textual criticism and exegesis that emerges from the first verse of Mark—which may serve as an example of innumerable other cases—is well and succinctly described in the text-critical/exegetical analysis of Mark 1:1 by Adela Yarbro Collins. She correctly asserts that, in the New Testament,

> the opening units of the actual texts provide important signals about the genre of the work as a whole and crucial information about the author's intention. The *incipit* of the Gospel of Mark (1:1) characterizes either the following text-unit or, more likely, the Gospel as a whole as "The beginning of the Gospel of Jesus Christ [son of God]." The question of the presence or absence of the words characterizing Jesus Christ as (the) son of God is important for the reasons just stated and for the question of how the theme of the identity of Jesus unfolds from the point of view of the reader.[16]

Yarbro Collins's own answer, after careful analyses of the external attestation, the internal evidence, and what she refers to as "the study of the historical context," is typical of difficult cases, for finally she must invoke the "balance of probabilities" procedure and deal with bundles of evidence that compete with one another, some pulling in one direction, others in another, and then venture what appears to be the most reasonable decision. More specifically in this instance, two readings emerge as candidates for the earliest reading, and—of those two—for her the external evidence "slightly favors" the reading with "Son of God," while the reading without "Son of God" is more easily accredited as the source for the reading that includes the phrase (rather than the reverse). At the same time, however, in her judgment other aspects of internal criticism (transcriptional probabilities beyond merely asking which reading best explains the other[s]) and matters of historical context (including influence from early christological controversies) "tip the scales" in favor of the reading without "Son of God."[17] It is the latter reading, presumably, that Yarbro Collins will exegete in her forthcoming Hermeneia commentary on Mark.

This summary of one exegete's careful examination of a range of considerations that enter into a "text-critical" decision shows that drawing a conclusion about which text to interpret is much broader than a mechanical application of certain "criteria" or "principles" of textual criticism. Rather, the immediate and larger context of the writing itself and of the historical-theological setting from which it arose and in which it later functioned may all be relevant factors in deciding between/among variant readings. Very often these cases are difficult, and all too frequently judgments must be made in the absence of full confidence.

An Example from Jesus' Sayings on Divorce and Remarriage

An occasional variation-unit relevant to the larger theme of this book—the role of women in the early Christian community— shows difficulties so bewildering that textual critics can only "throw up their hands" in despair of ever isolating what might be referred to as one, single "original" reading. One such case involves the tangled complex of textual variation in the Gospel passages reporting the sayings of Jesus on divorce and remarriage, which have been explored recently in a realistic fashion by David C. Parker in his often unsettling but always forward-looking book *The Living Text of the Gospels* (1997).[18] Parker devotes an entire chapter to an analysis of the variation units in the pericopae on divorce/remarriage in Mark 10:2–12; Matt 5:27–32; 19:3–9; and Luke 16:18. In a preliminary discussion on the degree of care shown by scribes in transmitting Gospel material, Parker points out (contrary to a common impression) that the number of textual variants "rises dramatically" in sayings passages over against those in narrative passages. He astutely asserts that the reason for this textual complexity in sayings of Jesus "is precisely the importance accorded to them,"[19] and I would add that one aspect of their importance was their relevance and applicability to the everyday, real-life issues in the Christian communities, whether spiritual or social in nature. Further, with respect to the common debate "whether the earliest Christians were *able* to pass on accurately the traditions (specifically, the teaching of Jesus)," Parker turns this conventional question on its head and

affirmed that "the real question is why they chose *not* to"[20]—
an issue to be treated further in a moment. Another insight of
Parker on the relationship of textual criticism to exegesis is worthy of emphasis:

> It is necessary at the outset to recognize how much higher
> the text-critical stakes have become. The assumption that
> Jesus issued specific, verbally precise commandments on
> certain matters is deeply seated. And this assumption has
> demanded that textual critics deliver the original specific,
> precise wording spoken by Jesus and recorded by the evan-
> gelists. But this is to prejudge the issue. First the evidence
> must be collected and scrutinised. Then conclusions will
> be drawn, and the legislators will have to make what they
> can of what they are given.[21]

Parker then points out that not only are there differences among
the three Gospels that record these divorce/remarriage sayings,
but there are variations also in each Gospel's manuscript tradition of the passage—differences sometimes "greater than those
between our printed Gospels"[22]—and as a result the varying
forms of Jesus' sayings on the subject number twenty. There is
no time here to review Parker's thorough text-critical analysis
of these variation-units, except to note a few points and then his
conclusions. The brief description that follows of necessity over-
looks much of the detailed textual variation and thereby over-
simplifies matters considerably, and Parker's discussion merits
careful reading for the full impact of the larger issues with which
he is concerned, some of which we shall highlight.

The distinctive feature of all Markan variant readings in 10:10–
12 is that, even in this oldest Gospel, the saying shows adaptation
to (and therefore formulation by) the Roman Christian community, for it envisions a woman divorcing her husband (something
not possible in Judaism), and in Mark adultery is "divorcing
one's spouse and remarrying," with some differing emphases in
the half-dozen textual variations—e.g., in most readings remarriage constitutes adultery, though in one variant divorce itself is
adultery for a man.[23] The situation in Matthew is quite different,
with the result that "Matthew and Mark are dealing with two
completely separate issues."[24] In view of the clause, "except for
porneia (adultery)" in both Matt 5:32 and 19:9, "the point is that

divorcing one's wife is to treat her as though she were an adulter-
ess"[25] (even if she were not), though the longer reading in three
other variations (stating that adultery is committed by marry-
ing a divorced woman) again focuses on the man and/or might
be an assertion of a woman's right to remain single—"to pro-
tect vulnerable people who wished not to remarry."[26] The Lukan
tradition is more unified and, like Mark, focuses on adultery
consisting in remarriage by men or women, though one variant
speaks only of the man's remarriage as adultery.[27]

Parker's conclusions in face of the twenty textual variations in
these passages are pointed and, to some, they may sound harsh:
"The recovery of a definitive 'original' text that is consequently
'authoritative' cannot be presumed to be an attainable target."
"The main result of this survey is to show that the recovery of a
single original saying of Jesus is impossible." "What we have is a
collection of interpretive rewritings of a tradition."[28] A distinct
advantage of this realism and honesty about the textual situation here (and in other comparable places) is that, as Parker says,
we are pressed to consider not one, but *all forms of the text*, for
the sayings on divorce/remarriage have taken on "a life of their
own" over time in various Christian communities.[29] Hence, we
must recognize that most of the textual variants in these groups
of sayings arose out of specific settings in early Christianity and
we must view "all the text forms as interpretations of the tradition."[30] However, after studying this manifold tradition and
learning from it "the divergent interpretations of early Christianity," still "the people of God have to make up their own minds.
There is no [single] authoritative text to provide a short-cut."[31]

The result for textual criticism from such a hard case as this, and
from other similar (if less complex) instances, has been twofold.
On the one hand, there now appears to be an increasing skepticism
about the validity of certain methods and about some of the "criteria" for the originality of readings, and also about the certainty
of results;[32] on the other hand, however, some forward-looking
scholars, such as Parker and Bart Ehrman, are attempting to make
a virtue out of adversity by asserting and then demonstrating that
certain intractable text-critical cases actually open for us a window on the struggles and insights of the early church that can, in
turn, enlighten the Christian community in our own time.[33] I also

have offered the bold and paradoxical principle that *the greater the ambiguity in the variant readings of a given variation unit, the more clearly we are able to grasp the concerns of the early church*.[34]

A Loss of Innocence

In view of all of this, it is fair to say that what our present situation signifies is a loss of innocence by New Testament textual criticism in recent times, and this has immediate implications for both textual critics and exegetes. For one thing, the nature of textual criticism as *both* art *and* science precludes any simple, mechanical application of "rules" or "principles" for determining the priority of readings—that is, the old "canons of criticism" can be counted on only rarely to yield a purely "objective" result. Useful, rather, are the "artful" skills of judgment in selecting the reading that best explains all others in a variation unit; interpretive dexterity in showing a reading's conformity to a writing's style or theology or a reading's derivation from an extraneous context; and the adroitness and sensitivity to explain how a reading has been formed or altered by church-historical pressures. These and other *internal arguments* for the priority of readings are crucial in the process, though some have come under scrutiny in recent decades, particularly the venerable argument that the shorter reading is preferable.[35] On the other hand, the *external arguments*, namely, the more clearly empirical measures—such as the age and provenance of manuscripts or determinations of their relative scribal quality—are often inadequate by themselves to accredit one reading over another because of our imperfect knowledge of the history of our transmitted New Testament text and our limited understanding of how the various manuscripts (the vehicles of transmission) are related to one another. In addition, the application of both the external and internal arguments for the priority of readings often will result in conflict, when, for example, the "harder reading" (i.e., the rougher or less elegant reading) may very well compete with a reading more in keeping with the author's literary style and vocabulary or theology, or with a reading in the more ancient witnesses. Then, as textual critics say (and as illustrated above), the "balance of probabilities" comes into play—the art of weighing various relevant arguments against one another and making a reasonable decision, that is, a contextual, qualitative judgment in which aspects of both "art" and "science" participate.

But is not this the situation in which textual criticism has long found itself? Yes, but that is exactly the point in what I have referred to as a "recent loss of innocence." If New Testament textual critics long ago had not only recognized these ambiguities and uncertainties in method (as they often did) but also had been able to move quickly, if not dramatically, toward their resolution, it would be different. As it is, however, textual criticism has been unable to refine either its internal arguments for priority of readings or its history of the New Testament text much beyond their status at the time of Westcott-Hort, and this languishing in ambiguities for more than a hundred years is what—it seems to me—has opened the door to a fair measure of skepticism and pessimism about developing unambiguous methods and achieving clear results. Hence, there is, among many, a loss of innocence and a recognition that the discipline may have to live out a further extended period of "balancing the probabilities" within a framework of frustrating uncertainties that includes competing "canons" of priority, conflicting external evidence, and multivalence in the term "original." Yet, just as the present situation in textual criticism has both its downside and its upside—skepticism about traditional methods alongside creative new approaches—so future work in the discipline presents itself as twofold: while encouraging explorations that might yield refinements and advances in text-critical methodology, New Testament textual criticism must also exploit the constructive possibilities opened recently by those who have begun to rethink our basic tasks and goals, with the expectation that unexplored and sometimes risky paths can now be pursued in an environment of free inquiry. I, for one, therefore project a bright and exciting (if perhaps somewhat tumultuous) future for the text-critical enterprise and, as an accompaniment, an enriching influence on exegesis.

2

VARIANT READINGS IN PASSAGES CONCERNING GENDER ISSUES

THE RELATIONSHIP BETWEEN textual criticism and exegesis, as noted earlier, might be demonstrated in any number of New Testament passages or by selecting any noteworthy theme of one or more New Testament writings. Indeed, the latter approach is often both interesting and instructive, especially when an issue is of contemporary concern in scholarship and/or for the church. Such studies, recent and older, include investigations, for example, like that of Bart D. Ehrman on early Christology[1] or analyses of Jewish-Christian relations in relevant passages that contain textual variation[2] or assessments of the authorship, thought, and nature of the Acts of the Apostles in view of the substantially different textual traditions in which it has been transmitted.[3] My original proposal for this project was to consider several passages involving gender issues where textual variation affects exegesis, a topic certainly of current significance—and controversy. For example, the tangle of variant readings in the divorce/remarriage sayings discussed above defies the isolation of a single "original" reading, thereby showing, à la David Parker, that the church lived, worked, and wrestled with several "interpretive rewritings of a tradition": "the early church rewrote the sayings in their attempt to make sense of them."[4] Because of this kind of text-critical situation, exegetes now are able to view and to interpret—through the several differing and sometimes competing variants—the ways in which one issue of special concern to women was being debated and was exerting pressure in the early centuries of Christianity. This result may not be as "clean" or as satisfying as seizing upon a single variant as "original," but it is both more realistic and more practical, that is, more likely consonant with the real-life situations of the early Christian community and therefore more

14

easily applicable to present-day Christianity, in which varying approaches to divorce and remarriage have surfaced and have been applied across the array of our Christian communities. As Parker is fond of saying (though this is a free paraphrase), the multiplicity of texts in the manuscript tradition enriches us as never before because we possess more than a single "original" reading would offer. Rather, we are open to instruction from all meaningful multiple variants that issue from the "living text of the gospels" and that bring to view the ways that the early church dealt with some of its serious concerns.[5] And, we might add, whenever the diverse manuscript tradition offers a range of possibilities that correspond to a multifaceted human problem, the living text resonates with that real living situation, so that fresh insights and productive resolutions may emerge.

First Corinthians 14:34–35 as Interpolation

A second passage that I had hoped to treat at length is 1 Cor 14:34–35. I had planned to argue—as several have done so effectively in recent years—that text-critical evidence supports the conclusion that this "silencing of women" pericope was not part of Paul's 1 Corinthians and perhaps not Pauline at all. Of course, many exegetes and textual critics defend its authenticity, including Joël Delobel, whose two-page discussion is a superb model of a text-critical analysis that is not only succinct and precise but at the same time comprehensive in covering the relevant evidence and issues—and therefore compelling in so many respects. In addition, I agree with and take seriously his counsel that, in "the present concern for the situation of man and woman in the church . . . contemporary concern should not decide whether or not a statement *can* be pauline."[6] However, some new evidence text-critical in nature may justify moving in the direction earlier suggested, and a brief summary of this new argumentation follows a review of the problem.

The well-known paragraph in 1 Cor 14:34–35 contains words long disturbing to many, both men and women, but most grievously to women committed to and desirous of service in the church, namely, "Women should be silent in the churches," followed by a further statement of submission to husbands and a reinforcement of silence by asserting that "it is shameful for a woman to speak in church." Neither here nor elsewhere, however, are words offensive to some merely to be whisked away; rather, critical analysis and scholarly methods must be applied and the results scrutinized—even if reasonable critics disagree on their interpretation. Here, however, I can provide only a sketch of this particular textual/exegetical crux. Note the passage, with its immediately preceding and following context (1 Cor 14:31–40):

> [31]For you can all prophesy one by one, so that all may learn and all be encouraged. [32]And the spirits of prophets are subject to the prophets, [33]for God is a God not of disorder but of peace.
>
> (As in all the churches of the saints, [34]women should be silent in the churches. For they are not permitted to speak, but should be subordinate, as the law also says. [35]If there is anything they desire to know, let them ask their husbands at home. For it is shameful for a woman to speak in church. [36]Or did the word of God originate with you? Or are you the only ones it has reached?)
>
> [37]Anyone who claims to be a prophet, or to have spiritual powers, must acknowledge that what I am writing to you is a commandment of the Lord. [38]Anyone who does not recognize this is not to be recognized. [39]So, my friends, be eager to prophesy, and do not forbid speaking in tongues; [40]but all things should be done decently and in order. (NRSV, which contains the parentheses)

Hans Conzelmann compressed into a single brief and terse paragraph the major factors that compelled him and other interpreters to designate 1 Cor 14:34–35 (he includes vv. 33b–36) a (non-Pauline) interpolation, though he provided also summaries of views that defended its authenticity. The factors favoring interpolation include the judgment that the section "upsets the context" by interrupting the theme of prophecy and by spoiling the flow of thought; that its content contradicts 1 Cor 11:2ff.; that it contains non-Pauline language and thought; and that v. 37 links not with v. 36 but with v. 33a.[7] Gordon Fee, in two separate ten-page treatments of 14:34–35, provided a masterfully thorough and incisive text-critical and exegetical analysis of both sides and all aspects of the issue. While fairly presenting opposing views, his own firm conclusion was that the passage is a non-Pauline interpolation—doubtless an early marginal gloss incorporated into the text at two different places (i.e., in their position as vv. 34–35 and after v. 40, where the D-text and other witnesses placed it).[8] A growing number of other scholars have argued recently for the interpolation view.[9]

On the other hand, Delobel's classic statement defending the authenticity of the passage on text-critical grounds may be taken as representative of the traditional view, held by many textual critics and exegetes.[10] Among other points, he emphasized that 1 Cor 14:34–35 is present in all extant manuscripts (even if differently placed by some) and that this overwhelming external evidence strongly favors authenticity; that any contradiction of views on women's silence here and in 1 Cor 11:2–16 is only apparent; and that moving vv. 34–35 to a position after v. 40 can be explained as a copyist's rather modest reaction to the *apparent* conflict with 11:2ff.[11] My question is whether textual criticism offers any additional assistance in solving this exegetical problem.

At first blush, a negative answer might be expected, for (as noted) these two verses are present in the entire textual tradition; hence, there is no divided manuscript tradition and there are no textual variants in the usual sense. However, as intimated above, a group of Greek-Latin bilingual manuscripts, D[Paul], F[Paul], and G[Paul]; other so-called Western (D-text) witnesses (ar, b, d, f, g); and two Latin church writers, Ambrosiaster and Sedulius Scotus, as well as the non-D-text minuscule 88,[12] place vv. 34–35 after v. 40. This dislocation in the textual tradition discloses some uncertainty among scribes as to where might be the appropriate place for vv. 34–35, or it may indicate a more serious question—do they belong in the letter at all? This hint from the D-text looms larger when it is noticed that vv. 34–35 invariably were treated as a separate paragraph—that is, not connected with v. 33b—in numerous major majuscules (manuscripts written in upper-case letters), including 𝔓46, ℵ, B, A, D[Paul], a number of minuscules (manuscripts written in lower-case letters), such as 33, and Origen.[13]

In addition, though vv. 34–35 were in their usual position in the Latin Codex Fuldensis (F, dated 547), the original scribe placed a siglum after v. 33 that referred the reader to a body of text in the bottom margin, namely, vv. 36–40 recopied in toto. As Philip B. Payne has shown, vv. 36–40 in the margin and its accompanying textual markings are most naturally understood as intended to replace vv. 34–40 above, with the net effect of removing vv. 34–35 from the text while retaining vv. 36–40. The scribe, or more properly Bishop Victor, who identified himself as the editor of Codex Fuldensis, apparently had textual evidence, as is apparent from all of his other emendations of the manuscript, that vv. 34–35 were not part of the text of 1 Corinthians.[14]

But the most significant data came from Payne's investigation of Codex Vaticanus (B, fourth century), whose original scribe employed distinctive sigla to mark vv. 34–35 as a known textual problem, which strongly supports the view that vv. 34–35 constituted an interpolation and was not Pauline at all.[15] The fascinating detail of Payne's analysis involves the aforementioned sigla, a series of some 765 pairs of dots (like a dieresis or umlaut) revealing a pattern that supports the notion that they mark lines of text differing from some other manuscripts; indeed, textual variants in such lines are far more frequent than lines without them.[16] Moreover, twenty-seven times umlauts in Codex B are accompanied by a horizontal line, half extending into the margin and placed below and to the right of the umlaut (hence, a "bar-umlaut"); and twelve additional times such a bar is on the left of a column with its umlaut on the right (hence a separated bar-umlaut). Payne provides more than sufficient evidence to show that these bar-umlauts also are "sigla indicating textual problems,"[17] and he notes (a) that a separated bar-umlaut stands at the end of John 7:52 (which is followed immediately by 8:12—Vaticanus does not have the famous *pericope adulterae*, 7:53—8:11), doubtless an indicator of variation from other manuscripts; and (b) that a bar-umlaut separates 1 Cor 14:33 from 14:34, giving a similar signal.[18]

This was the situation for 1 Cor 14:34–35 around 1995, but after the appearance of P. B. Payne's study that year, it had been asserted that the umlauts "postdate the fourteenth century, probably belonging to the sixteenth" and that "Vaticanus, therefore, does not attest a fourth-century omission of the passage,"[19] but Payne, with Paul Canart, professor of paleography at the Vatican, examined Codex B with a high-powered lighted magnifying glass and were able to demonstrate conclusively that eleven umlauts "unambiguously match the original apricot color of unreinforced text on the same page of the codex," and that nine of these "mark a location where text is omitted, inserted or replaced in other manuscripts."[20] "Unreinforced text" refers to words or marks that were missed or omitted by a scribe (ninth to eleventh centuries) who traced over every letter of Codex B with chocolate-brown ink, so at least the eleven that match the original ink were made by the original scribe. A strong case can be made that the remaining umlauts were also original rather than introduced at the time the text was traced, but the point for our 1 Cor 14:34–35 passage is more easily made, for Canart detected a small protrusion of apricot-like ink from the chocolate-brown tracing, providing a high degree of assurance that the textual alert at vv. 34–35 was the work of the first scribe—and, therefore, grounds for interpreting that signal as a pointer to the passage being an interpolation.[21]

In 2003 another unsuccessful attempt was made to refute the view that the umlaut siglum in Codex B at 1 Cor 14:34–35 indicates an interpolation,[22] but again Philip Payne quickly and adroitly demonstrated that the effort was ill-founded and that the special mark (along with others) in Vaticanus functioned as he and Canart had argued.[23]

Finally, a case has been made recently that minuscule 88, which places 1 Cor 14:34–35 after 14:40, was copied from a Greek manuscript that did not contain vv. 34–35.[24]

In this striking example, we observe how exegesis—numerous scholars viewing 1 Cor 14:34–35 as disruptive of its immediate and larger context[25]—alerts us to a text-critical problem, and how textual criticism, in turn, assists us in a solution to the exegetical difficulty. And this combination of literary analysis and text-critical assessment has moved a sizable group of scholars to view the passage on "silent women" as a later intrusion into 1 Corinthians and most likely one never written by Paul.

This is a brief summary of a few explorations relevant to my theme, although the special significance of the 1 Corinthians passage will be highlighted in due course. I turn now to a crucial passage that has been the focus of discussion and controversy, especially in the last decade or two, and one that reveals—perhaps surprisingly, perhaps not—a pervasive sociocultural bias that has operated in New Testament textual criticism and exegesis for an entire century of what we might have regarded as the period of our most modern, liberal, and detached scholarly inquiry. Let us see how this lamentable story unfolds and how irony and paradox accompany its development.

⌗ ⌗ ⌗ ⌗ ⌗

PART II

JUNIA/JUNIAS
IN ROMANS 16:7

IF PAUL DID not insist on women keeping silent in the churches, might he also recognize a woman as an apostle? During the past few decades Rom 16:7 has been recognized as of pivotal importance in determining what leadership roles women assumed in earliest Christianity. This case is of special interest also because of the striking changes over some seventeen centuries in the way this passage has been understood, including—for a significant portion of that time—an interpretation that obviously reflects gender bias. In very recent times, as this bias has been exposed and, in a limited fashion, overcome, Rom 16:7 has been chief among several passages prominent in the exploration of and debate over the appropriateness of full ordination for women in various Christian communions, for this text—depending on the linguistic, text-critical, and exegetical decisions made—offers the one place where Paul used the word "apostle" to describe a woman.

Since the last chapter of Paul's letter to the Romans is read only rarely, it is helpful to recognize that, like the closing of virtually all letters in the Greco-Roman period, it contains mostly greetings—in this case, from Paul to specific Christians in Rome who were known to him. More than two dozen people are sent greetings: seventeen men and eight women, but—as pointed out frequently—those described as contributing most to the churches are *seven women but only five men*, and Prisca, a woman, is listed ahead of Aquila, her husband.[1] Also, at the outset of the chapter, Phoebe is introduced as a "deacon." In the midst of these greetings is verse 7, in which Paul requested his readers to:

> Greet Andronicus and Ἰουνιαν [literally, "Iunian" or
> "Junian"], my relatives [or "compatriots"] who were in
> prison with me; they are prominent among the apostles
> and they were in Christ before I was. (NRSV, but retaining
> the Greek of the disputed name, Junia/Junias)

What we have here are Andronicus, a man, and either Junia, a
woman, or Junias, a man—depending (allegedly) on how the second name is accented in Greek, but both persons are described as
"outstanding [or noteworthy] among the apostles." If the second
individual is a woman, then Junia is presented here as the first
and only woman to be called "apostle" in the canonical writings
of New Testament.[2]

One might say that this example involves the mere difference of a Greek accent in a proper name, but, as we shall see,
the matter is by no means as simple as that, for there are extensive complications, not only text-critical and exegetical, but
also cultural-hermeneutical in nature.

⌘ ⌘ ⌘ ⌘ ⌘
3

THE LEXICAL FORM
AND INTRODUCTORY MATTERS

THE ACCUSATIVE SINGULAR form Ἰουνιαν can be either the feminine Ἰουνίαν (from Ἰουνία, -ας, ἡ, "Junia") or masculine. The latter could take two forms (as has been postulated), either Ἰουνιᾶν (from Ἰουνιᾶς, -ᾶ, ὁ, "Junias"), or Ἰουνίαν (from Ἰουνίας, -α, ὁ, "Junias"), both of which would be nouns of the first declension. However, these two alleged masculine forms, though perhaps more often the former, have customarily been understood as shortened forms of the Greek name Ἰουνιανός (Junianos)[1] or the Latin name *Iunianus*, but this is a complex subject to be discussed more fully as we go along. It may be said at the outset, however, that "Junia" (feminine) is the easiest and most natural reading of Ἰουνιαν for several reasons:

a. Junia was a common Roman name for either noble members of the *gens Junia* (the clan of Junia) or for freed slaves of the *gens* (or their descendants)—with the freed slaves more numerous than the nobles.[2]

b. Junia was how Ἰουνιαν was understood whenever discussed by ancient Christian writers of late antiquity "without exception."[3]

c. Ἰουνίαν (so accented) was the reading of Greek New Testaments from Erasmus in 1516 to Erwin Nestle's edition of 1927[13] (with the exception of Alford in 1852) and during that period no alternate reading (i.e., Ἰουνιᾶν) appears to have been offered in any apparatus (except Weymouth [1892]) (see Tables 1 and 2 below, pages 62–63).

d. "All extant early translations (Old Latin, Vulgate, Sahidic and Bohairic Coptic, and Syriac versions) without exception transcribe the name in what can be taken as a feminine form; none gives any positive sign that a masculine name is being transcribed."[4]

e. The feminine Junia is how Rom 16:7 was read in English translations of the New Testament from Tyndale (1526/1534) almost without exception (see Dickinson, 1833, and Table 3, below) until the last quarter of the nineteenth century.

f. Neither of the alleged masculine forms of the name Junias has been found anywhere.

g. The hypothesis of Junias as a contracted name has serious problems.

Clearly, Junia is the prima facie choice and one that does not require the legerdemain that has long been employed to accredit one or the other masculine reading.

The masculine forms, for reasons (f) and (g) just mentioned, as well as others, have numerous attendant difficulties. Symptomatic of the problem is the fact that, until the mid-1990s, there was (to my knowledge) no extended discussion (and never any detailed defense) of the masculine forms or of the contracted name theory for this specific name, Junias. Rather, interpreters, for nearly a century now, merely repeated what two standard reference works (and their predecessors) had long *suggested* about the origin of the masculine name, Junias, in order to legitimate it, namely, Walter Bauer's lexicon and Friedrich Blass's grammar. These works invoked the contracted name phenomenon of the Greco-Roman world, but when they applied it to Junias they did so with caution, for Bauer described the name as "probably" shortened from Iunianus, while Blass placed a question mark after his suggestion of the same possibility.[5] Numerous interpreters who followed them dropped the caution and assumed the validity of the theory. The issue, more specifically then, is whether Ἰουνιᾶς, -ᾶ, ὁ, or Ἰουνίας, -α, ὁ, ever existed as Greco-Roman names and, if so, whether such masculine forms can be demonstrated to be contractions of Junianus. The first question, though I shall come back to it, has been answered above (and in many recent commentaries and articles): the masculine forms are nowhere attested (except of course by inference from the unaccented accusative form Ἰουνιαν in Rom 16:7, which, however, would be the accusative singular for both alleged masculine forms, just as it is for the feminine Ἰουνία).

As to the second question—whether Junias is a contracted name—older reference works, including the predecessors of Blass-Debrunner's grammar and Bauer's lexicon, tended to mention only Ἰουνίας (-α, ὁ), though occasionally both masculine forms were invoked.[6] More recently, however, the current lexica and grammars, as well as virtually all current commentators and authors of articles who broach the issue, take Ἰουνιᾶς (-ᾶ, ὁ) as the term to be discussed as the likely masculine name behind Junias. Moreover, the only evidence adduced to support Junias as a contracted name comes *by analogy* with similar names ending in –ᾶς, which are numerous enough[7] and three of which happen to occur in the Romans 16 list, namely, Πατροβᾶς, Patrobas (from Πατρόβιος, Patrobios)[8] and Ἑρμᾶς, Hermas (perhaps from Ἑρμόδωρος, Hermodoros) in Rom 16:14, and Ὀλυμπᾶς, Olympas (perhaps from Ὀλυμπιόδωρος, Olympiodoros)[9] in Rom 16:15. Yet, that does not answer specifically whether Ἰουνιᾶς is the result of such a contraction (see the further discussion below).

The terrain is much more murky with respect to the alleged masculine Ἰουνίας, -α, ὁ. Indeed, this instance typifies the frustration attendant upon the entire Junia/Junias matter, for as far as I can determine (except for one highly doubtful case to be treated in due course), no one has offered any evidence for the actual existence of this masculine name, either its occurrence in another literary text, an inscription, or a documentary source, or—which would be preferable and more convincing—in a specifically masculine context or in a masculine grammatical construction (e.g., with an accompanying relative pronoun) or the like. Moreover, I have been unable to discover any discussion at all of the name Ἰουνίας (Junias) by those who employ it. Rather, what has happened is that the name tended occasionally to crop up in a reference work or in a discussion as a *given*—something asserted as a kind of self-authenticating name. For example, J. B. Lightfoot asserted it as masculine in connection with the English Revised Version (RV) New Testament of 1881, where the masculine name Junias occurred in this influential new English version; presumably it was a translation of Ἰουνίαν (so accented), the reading of the Oxford Greek text of the same year that purportedly provided the Greek basis for the RV. Lightfoot, in an

1871 volume prepared in view of the revision work for the RV, stated:

> It seems probable that we should render the name Ἰουνίαν, one of S. Paul's kinsfolk, who was "noted among the apostles" (Rom. xvi.7) by Junias (*i.e.* Junianus), not Junia.[10]

He offers this with no overt reason, though the rationale lies subtly in the quotation itself: "noted among the apostles" (as will be discussed below). Somewhat later, William Sanday and Arthur C. Headlam mentioned the masculine form after the Rom 16:7 *lemma*, Ἰουνίαν, as follows: "there is some doubt as to whether this name is masculine, Ἰουνίας or Ἰουνιᾶς, a contraction of Junianus, or feminine, Junia";[11] M.-J. Lagrange reported both masculine forms, noting that one or the other might possibly be a contracted form of *Iunianus* from its Greek form Ἰουνιάνος (though he concludes that it is more prudent to take the name as feminine);[12] and, as a final example, in their prominent concordance, William F. Moulton and Albert S. Geden[13] placed Ἰουνίας at the head of the entry listing Ἰουνίαν from Rom 16:7.

The frustrating aspect of the alleged masculine name Ἰουνίας (which is not the case with Ἰουνιᾶς) is that it permits an interpreter to claim that the accusative Ἰουνίαν, whenever it appears in accented manuscripts or anywhere else in a discussion of Rom 16:7, is masculine, when, of course, it could just as well—and more naturally—be feminine. If the only alleged masculine form were Ἰουνιᾶς, however, then the way the accusative form Ἰουνιαν was accented would make it clear at once whether the feminine (Ἰουνίαν), or masculine (Ἰουνιᾶν) was understood or intended.

In this connection, it is curious that Kurt Aland's concordance, under the entry Ἰουνιᾶς (masculine), contained the added note that the Greek New Testaments of Heinrich J. Vogels, Hermann von Soden, Constantin Tischendorf, B. F. Westcott and F. J. A. Hort, and Charles Lloyd (1873 *textus receptus*) have the name Ἰουνίας,[14] the presumed alternate masculine form. These five editions, of course, all have Ἰουνίαν—which could be the accusative form of either the feminine Ἰουνία or of the alleged

masculine Ἰουνίας, so the question naturally arises: If a masculine name Ἰουνίας actually had existed, how could one know
the gender intended by Ἰουνίαν in these critical editions—especially when all other Greek New Testaments from Erasmus in
1516 through the Nestle edition of 1923[12], including Karl Lachmann, Samuel P. Tregelles, Richard F. Weymouth, Bernhard
Weiss, Alexander Souter, and eleven other editions of Nestle, also
print Ἰουνίαν in their texts (with the exception, already noted,
of Henry Alford; see Tables 1 and 2, below)? Of course, the question is moot if it should turn out that Ἰουνίας is not a viable
masculine name.

It is important to emphasize, however, that the identification
of Ἰουνίαν as Junia does not depend on proving the nonexis-
tence of the masculine name Ἰουνίας. Even if a dozen instances
of the latter suddenly should turn up in first-century papyri,
Junia would still be the most natural and compelling translation of Ἰουνίαν in Rom 16:7. After all, the masculine Junias
(Ἰουνίας) was asserted (I would say invented) when no evidence for such a masculine name could be found, a circumstance
still unchanged, so if data supporting it were to be found, at most
we would have for the first time some basis for the long-standing
but hitherto unsupported Junias *hypothesis*, but that hypothesis
still would have to withstand the tests (a) of the contracted name
proposal, (b) of how Ἰουνίαν was understood in the early centuries of Christianity, and (c) of the context in Romans 16 (see
below on all of these).

So, with Ἰουνίας (masculine) in the picture, puzzlement
increases and frustration is pervasive. Yet, there are several
instances in which we can know for sure or be reasonably certain about the gender that was intended or at least understood
when Ἰουνίαν (so accented) was found in a Greek critical edition or was translated for a version. We do know, of course, that
the translators of the KJV understood the Ἰουνίαν of the *textus
receptus* to mean Junia, for that is how they translated the term.
That is good evidence, though not absolute proof that the trans-
mitters of the *textus receptus* so understood it. More to the point,
we do know absolutely how Erasmus understood the Ἰουνίαν
he printed in his 1516 Greek New Testament, for his *Annotations*

on the New Testament, which were first published in 1516 along with that edition, contained the following annotation on the Rom 16:7 Vulgate *lemma, Andronicum et Iuliam:*

> 'Ιουνίαν, that is, "Junia." He [Paul] gives Julia her own place later on [Rom 16:15].

In 1527, Erasmus inserted an addition to this note:

> The very old codex furnished from the church of Constance agreed with the Greek manuscripts.[15]

Although the Vulgate Erasmus used in 1516 had *Iuliam,* understood by Erasmus as "Julia" (as his note clearly showed), he preferred the reading found in Greek, namely "Junia." The Vulgate of 1527 read *Iuniam,* corresponding to Erasmus's choice of "Junia." Much later, the Wordsworth-White critical text of the Vulgate (1913) left no doubt in its apparatus that what "all Greek" manuscripts had was 'Ιουνίαν, and that this was the equivalent of the Latin *Iuniam* in the critical text.[16] We have been careful up to this point not to equate *Iuniam* and "Junia" automatically (as Erasmus does), even though one might think that *Iuniam* would be "Junia" here and everywhere else, but see the excursus on Latin masculine/feminine accusatives, below.

As another example, we may consider the Greek Testament that Eberhard Nestle followed (for his first three editions) when Tischendorf and Westcott-Hort differed, namely, R. F. Weymouth's influential *Resultant Greek Testament* (1892, 1905³).[17] Weymouth printed 'Ιουνίαν as his text, and, again, we know assuredly that he understood this as feminine, for his English version, *The New Testament in Modern Speech* (1903),[18] which was made from the text of his *Resultant Greek Testament,* had "Junia." The Westcott-Hort Greek Testament provides another example, though hardly as definitive; their edition had no apparatus and their "Notes on Select Readings" in the *Introduction* volume contained no reference to Rom 16:7, yet Hort's *preference* on Junia/Junias was clear enough from his 1895 *Prolegomena to St Paul's Epistles to the Romans and the Ephesians,* where (while including the less likely alternative) he referred to "Andronicus and Junia (or Junias)."[19] Obviously he preferred Junia.

An early example on the other side of the ledger is Benjamin Wilson's 1864 *Emphatic Diaglott Containing the Original Greek Text . . . with an Interlineary Word for Word English Translation*,[20] where, of course, the English makes explicit how the editor understood the Greek, and here Ἰουνίαν has been translated as "Junias."

Another method—though by no means a certain one—for determining how an editor of the Greek New Testament understood the gender of Ἰουνίαν is whether the alternate reading stood in the apparatus. For example, we have just noted Weymouth's *Resultant Greek Testament*, where the text read Ἰουνίαν; the apparatus here reported that Alford's *Greek Testament* (1844–1857) printed –ιᾶν, the distinctly masculine ending.[21] Weymouth might simply have been recording Alford's reading as the alternative *masculine* form, but we know (from the reference above to his English translation) that he was, in fact, noting Alford's masculine as opposed to his own feminine reading. When Alford's *Greek Testament* is itself examined, his notes were very clear, for Alford said explicitly that the name may be feminine, namely, Ἰουνίαν from Ἰουνία, or masculine (as in his text) from Ἰουνιᾶς.[22] Other cases are not so transparent. The Erwin Nestle editions from 1930[14] to 1952[21] and the Nestle-Aland editions from 1956[22] to 1963[25] all had Ἰουνιᾶν in the text, but stated in the apparatus that –ίαν was read by HTW, i.e., Westcott-Hort, Tischendorf, and Weiss. George Kilpatrick (BFBS, 1958[2]) also prints Ἰουνιᾶν as text, with –ίαν as the alternate reading. This does not necessarily mean that Kilpatrick and the Nestle/Nestle-Aland editions listed above intended to report that, while their own texts had "Junias," others opted for "Junia"; as mentioned already, they could have been indicating simply that the Greek for the masculine "Junias" had an alternative accentuation. But how likely is this? After all, the manuscripts most heavily relied upon and considered most important for the Greek New Testament, namely the papyri and majuscules, were seldom accented prior to the seventh century, so, in that situation, what were these and other editors who list the alternate reading –ίαν actually trying to convey to the users of their editions? Were they merely reporting a different accentuation for two masculine forms of the name, or were they showing that their reading of the masculine had a feminine alternative that was read by earlier and contemporary editions? On the face of it, the latter is much more likely, especially when it is recognized that the quest for the earliest text would not be affected in any definitive way simply by different accents in this word in texts later than the sixth or seventh centuries, and one wonders, therefore, why a mere difference in accent that would be relevant only for the later manuscripts of the New Testament tradition would be worth mentioning in the apparatus. It seems fair to conclude, then, that editions with the clearly masculine form Ἰουνιᾶν that then list –ίαν as the alternate reading understand the latter as the feminine name "Junia."

The Nestle-Aland and UBS editions will be treated at length later, though the situation we have been addressing would appear to have been clarified in UBS⁴ (1993), for here, though the text had Ἰουνιᾶν, the apparatus specifically—in these very words—separated "Ἰουνιᾶν (masculine)" from "Ἰουνίαν (feminine)." Of course, if Ἰουνίας is a viable masculine name, then it could still be argued that what is called "feminine" in the UBS apparatus should be viewed as mistaken and that the name could also be "masculine," though assuredly that is not what UBS intended to convey; rather, for the editors of the 1993 UBS⁴, there was one clearly masculine form (and not two) and one clearly feminine. I suggest that this newly found clarity regarding Ἰουνιαν represented a shift away from a masculine Ἰουνίας, a change that had been in process over recent years and had reached completion. The result is that only one masculine remains in the discussion, Ἰουνιᾶς, which was always clearly masculine, alongside the feminine Ἰουνία, with the further important result that Ἰουνίαν now represents only the feminine accusative (and no longer the masculine accusative). As intimated, such a shift has taken place not only in the 1993 UBS⁴ edition, but more generally *and already earlier* in scholarship on the subject, and this is evident, for example, in current reference works, such as BAGD, BDF, *IDB*, *ABD*, and *EDNT*, and in recent commentaries on Romans, such as those by Charles E. B. Cranfield (1979), James D. G. Dunn (1988), Joseph A. Fitzmyer (1993), and Douglas Moo

(1996), to mention merely a few, where only the two possibilities were envisioned—the feminine in –ίαν and the masculine in –ιᾶν. To be sure, Dunn alluded to Ἰουνίας by saying that the Rom 16:7 reading "Ἰουνίαν has usually been taken in the modern period as Ἰουνιᾶν" (a statement that is itself evidence of the shift just proposed), but then he dismisses the notion in favor of the meaning "Junia" for Ἰουνίαν. When further reasons are offered later in this volume for dispensing with Ἰουνίας as a legitimate contender, we should be able to say with considerable confidence that Ἰουνίαν means "Junia" (and Ἰουνιᾶν means "Junias"), and that this may hold not only for our own times but for the vast majority of Greek New Testaments of the past and for Greek manuscripts as well, that is, whenever accents appear in Ἰουνιαν. But this is to get ahead of my story.

I may summarize the problem to this point. At Rom 16:7 the same Greek word, Ἰουνιαν, occurs in all Greek manuscripts except for five that have a variant of another kind, namely, "Julia."[23] But Julia is clearly a woman's name—the most popular by far of all names in Rome,[24] and the variant's significance is simply that it supports the presence of a feminine name in the text, rather than a masculine. So my concern is with only one Greek word in only one form, Ἰουνιαν, an accusative singular most naturally of the feminine Ἰουνία or Junia. How, on any scheme, then, did scholars get to a masculine term and to a man Junias?

Before resuming the discussion of the proposed masculine forms of Ἰουνιαν, perspective will be gained by examining how the Junia/Junias matter was treated in the Christian writers of late antiquity, the Middle Ages, and the Reformation period. By way of anticipation, data from the several earliest centuries may permit us to argue that the early, unaccented manuscripts intended their Ἰουνιαν to refer to "Junia," since (as I am about to document) early church writers were unanimous in claiming "Junia" (or the likewise feminine "Julia") for Rom 16:7.

4

JUNIA IN EARLY CHRISTIAN
WRITERS—AND BEYOND

IN HIS COMMENTARY on Romans, Joseph A. Fitzmyer listed some sixteen Greek and Latin commentators of the first Christian millennium who understood Ἰουνιαν in Rom 16:7 as "Junia," feminine (sometimes "Julia" occurs), and often Junia was considered to be the wife of Andronicus.[1] These writers include Origen (ca. 185–254) as translated by Rufinus (345–410; see further below) and also as quoted by Rabanus Maurus (ca. 776–856); Ambrosiaster (ca. 375), though he uses Julia; John Chrysostom (ca. 344/354–407); Jerome (ca. 345–419); Theodoret of Cyrrhus (ca. 393–ca. 458); Ps.-Primasius (died ca. 567); John Damascene (ca. 675–ca. 749); Hraban of Fulda (780–856); Haymo of Halberstadt (fl. 840–853); Hatto of Vercelli (tenth century), who names Julia; Oecumenius (first half of the sixth century); Lanfranc of Bec (ca. 1005–1089); Bruno the Carthusian (ca. 1030–1101); Theophylact (fl. 1070–1081); Peter Abelard (1079–1142); and Peter Lombard (ca. 1095–1169). Linda Belleville adds the following Latin church writers: Ambrose (339–397); Claudius of Turin (d. 827); Sedulius-Scotus (fl. 848–858); Guillelmus Abbas (1085–1147/48); and Herveus Burgidolensis (late eleventh cent.–1151).[2]

By far the most influential of these, and among the earliest, was Chrysostom, whose statement is pointed and unambiguous:

> "Greet Andronicus and Junia . . . who are outstanding among the apostles": To be an apostle is something great. But to be outstanding among the apostles—just think what a wonderful song of praise that is! They were outstanding on the basis of their works and virtuous actions. Indeed, how great the wisdom of this woman must have been that she was even deemed worthy of the title of apostle. (*In ep. ad Romanos* 31.2; PG 60.669–670)[3]

In the next century, Theodoret (ca. 393–ca. 458), Bishop of Cyr-rhus, echoes the same sentiments in a less flamboyant statement in reference to Andronicus and Junia:

> Then to be called "of note" not only among the disciples but also among the teachers, and not just among the teach-ers but even among the apostles. (*Interpretatio in quatuor-decim epistolas S. Pauli* 82.200)[4]

Much later, the formulation of Chrysostom appears to find a new voice in John of Damascus (ca. 675–ca. 749):

> And to be called "apostles" is a great thing ... but to be even amongst these of note, just consider what a great encomium this is. (Commentary on Paul's Epistles 95.565)[5]

Earlier I asserted and provided some evidence that Junias, whether as Ἰουνίας or Ἰουνιᾶς, cannot be documented in the Greco-Roman world, at least to date—a view shared by many other recent writers on the subject.[6] This assertion is made in spite of two exceptions that have been alleged: (1) that Junias was mentioned by Origen according to Rufinus's Latin transla-tion of his commentary on Romans, and (2) that Epiphanius (315–403) thought of a male figure. However, every time these are mentioned—even by those whose views would benefit from such an identification—the claims are either dismissed or rea-sons to be cautious are cited.

Fortunately, in the case of the alleged reference to Junias in Rufinus's Latin translation of Origen's commentary on Romans, we now have the complete critical edition (except for the Greek fragments) by the late Caroline Hammond Bammel, with Ori-gen's comments on Rom 16:7 appearing in the volume published in 1998.[7] This context contained three references to *Andronicus et Iunia* in *In ep. ad Romanos* 10.21, lines 1, 10, and 25; there are no manuscript variants in these cases other than the usual *Iulia* ("Julia") in two different correctors' hands of a single manu-script. The accusative case appeared in lines 1 and 10: *Androni-cum et Iuniam*, while the ablative occurred in line 25: *Andronico et Iunia*. A fourth reference occurred in 10.39, line 45, this time in the nominative case: *Andronicus et Iunia*, with the latter sup-ported by two major manuscripts, W (eighth/ninth century) and

R (ninth), and a member of a subgroup, E (twelfth); the variant *Iulia* was read by the twelfth-century manuscript c. It is in this passage where the variant *Iunias* (nominative) occurred in two members of the subgroup of which E is a member, namely, f and e, both twelfth-century manuscripts. Hammond Bammel's critical text properly contains *Iunia* in all four instances—and on good authority, while *Iunias* is a variant in two out of three late manuscripts that belong to a single subgroup, grounds perhaps for asserting that this amounts really to one variant reading, not two. In any event, this alleged exception can be dismissed as carrying little if any weight, and we can be confident that Origen read Rom 16:7 as "Junia." By the way—in view of the excursus below on Latin masculine/feminine accusatives—the occurrences of *Iunia* in the nominative and ablative cases (in addition to the accusative found in Rom 16:7) are helpful, because there can be no doubt that feminine forms are used by Origen in these passages.

Finally, Rabanus Maurus (ca. 776–856), quoting Origen, had "Junia" also[8] and, in a section of Origen's commentary on Romans by Hraban of Fulda (780–856), which he took literally from Rufinus's Origen, the name Junia is to be read, not Junias.[9]

The alleged exception in Epiphanius arose from a electronic search of the *Thesaurus Linguae Graecae* for all *Greek* forms of Ἰουνια- by John Piper and Wayne Grudem, which turned up only three instances besides Rom 16:7, namely a Ἰουνία in Plutarch's *Life of Brutus* (7.1); the Ἰουνία reference in Chrysostom; and Ἰουνιας "of whom Paul makes mention" in Epiphanius (*Index disciplulorum*, 125.19–20), where the relative pronoun is masculine, indicating a male Junias. However, as Piper and Grudem themselves confess, in commendable candor, "We are perplexed about the fact that in the near context of the citation concerning Junias, Epiphanius also designates Prisca as a man mentioned in Romans 16:3, even though we know from the New Testament that she is a woman."[10] So, although Junias is represented in Epiphanius as male—which (ruling out the Origen/Rufinus instance) would then be the only such occurrence in late antiquity—the credibility of the witness is tarnished, with the result that this alleged exception is highly suspect. Hence I conclude, with a high degree of confidence, that to date a bona fide instance of Junias, whether in Greek or Latin, has not been found. Incidentally, Richard Cervin adds an instance of Ἰουνία (feminine) in Greek, which obviously is not the common name that it was in Latin, from an inscription mentioning Junia Torquata, known from the *Annals* of Tacitus (3.69).[11]

When we move from late antiquity to the late Middle Ages in our search for the male name Junias, we discover that Aegidius (or Giles) of Rome (ca. 1243/47–1316) is commonly credited as the first to identify Junia as male when he referred to the pair greeted in Rom 16:7 as "those honorable men [*viri*]." As Bernadette Brooten explained:

> Aegidius noted that there were two variant readings for the second name: *Juniam* and *Juliam* (accusative in the verse). He preferred the reading *Juliam* and took it to be masculine. Thus we see that even *Juliam*, which modern scholars would take to be clearly feminine, has been considered masculine in the context of the title "apostle."[12]

Thus, for Aegidius, Andronicus's partner (Julia or Julias?) also became male, and the impact of this interpretation (or similar ones) on future exegesis was by no means negligible.

A similar reading of *Iuniam* as masculine can be observed two centuries later—in a volume Brooten mentions in her article that has been on my shelf unopened for two decades: *S. Pauli epistolae XIV ex Vulgata, adiecta intelligentia ex graeco, cum commentariis* by Jacobus Faber Stapulensis (Jacques LeFèvre d'Étaples), 1512.[13] LeFèvre opened his comments on Romans 16 by reporting that Paul "salutes 20 holy men by name and 8 women" (the latter noted almost incidentally), and then lists each group; the men are "Aquila, Epaenetus, Andronicus, Julias [16:7] . . . Philologus, Julias [16:15], Nereus," while the list of women, of course, did not include Junia or Julia, who were already in the list of men.[14] But, what is striking is that in his more detailed comments LeFèvre did exactly what Erasmus would do four years later: present the Vulgate reading, *Andronicum & Iuliam*, then his preference in Latin, *Iuniam*, and finally the Greek (though, of course, there was no printed Greek Testament when LeFèvre

wrote): ἀνδρόνικον καὶ ἰουνίαν. The Vulgate of the time (as
for Erasmus) had "Julia," and (like Erasmus) LeFèvre preferred
the Greek Ἰουνίαν, but (unlike Erasmus in his *Annotations*)
LeFèvre explicitly took the accusative *Iuniam* as if from the
masculine nominative *Iunias* (just as, for him, in Rom 16:15 the
"Julia" of "Philologus and Julia" became "Julias"—something I
have not observed in any other writer; Erasmus, however, would
paraphrase this latter passage as "Greet Philologus and his wife
Julia"—where no ambiguity remained).[15]

✖ ✖ ✖

EXCURSUS
Latin Masculine/Feminine Accusatives

The possibility of taking *Iuniam* in Latin as masculine accusative
(as LeFèvre did, and as Aegidius did with *Iuliam*), when any Latin
reader (whether Erasmus or a modern student) might assume
that it clearly was the feminine accusative of *Iunia*, requires an
excursus. Indeed, once again we encounter a frustrating phenomenon that begs for explanation, but among writers on Rom 16:7
only Brooten in her allusion to "*Juliam*, which modern scholars
would take to be clearly feminine" (just quoted above) and John
Thorley in his linguistic discussion alerted us to the problem.
The most efficient way to present Thorley's well-argued position
is to quote a lengthy albeit concise paragraph:

> In the case of the Vulgate it must be said that any Latin
> reader would immediately take "Iuniam" to be a women's
> name. However, in considering the possibility that the
> Greek text might represent the accusative of a masculine
> name, it is necessary to review the Vulgate practice in tran-
> scribing from the Greek the accusative of masculine names
> that ended in the nominative in -ΑΣ; can ΙΟΥΝΙΑΜ,
> which can obviously be the accusative of a feminine name
> Junia, also represent the accusative of a supposed mascu-
> line name written in Greek as ΙΟΥΝΙΑΣ? The Sixtine edi-
> tion (1590) and the Clementine edition (1592) do not help
> here, since both editions standardised all such endings into
> a Latinised -AM, which could morphologically be a mas-

culine or a feminine form. But the manuscript tradition
does not justify this standardisation.[16]

Thus, Thorley argued that, since Wordsworth and White's Vulgate edition of 1911ff., the following "more complex pattern
based on the best manuscripts" has emerged, which he summarized under two points (though his many examples from the
New Testament are omitted here):

a. "The accusative of Greek masculine names ending in cir-
   cumflex accented –ᾶν (perispomenon) is *usually* written in
   Latin as -AN *if the name has more than two syllables.*" (Note
   the qualifier, *usually*; the only two exceptions include Patro-
   ba*m* in Rom 16:14.)

b. "However, the accusative of Greek masculine names with
   perispomenon accentuation *of two syllables* is written *always*
   in Latin as –AM."[17]

Since Iunia consists of more than two syllables and fits cat-
egory (a), Thorley's conclusion was that "one might have
expected 'Iunia*n*' if Jerome had thought the name was masculine; indeed such a spelling was *essential* in Latin if a man's name
was intended, in order to distinguish it from the common female
name."[18]

This analysis helps a great deal in understanding how the late
sixteenth century Vulgate editions, which had *Iuniam*, could
on occasion be read as masculine, though it would not be the
expected reading. I note that Greek-Latin New Testaments, such
as Bover (1968[5]) and Merk (1992[11]), who printed the Clementine
Vulgate of 1592, both adopted the Greek Ἰουνιᾶν (masculine)
parallel to their Latin *Iuniam*. That, however, does not necessarily mean that their clearly masculine Greek is due to their
reading of the Vulgate text—there are other explanations for
the Greek, as I have observed. On the other hand, perhaps in
confirmation of Thorley's data, I notice that Bonifatius Fischer,
the lamented director of the Vetus-Latina Institut in Beuron,
in his magisterial concordance to the Vulgate, used the *lemma
Iunia* (i.e., "Junia"), for the single biblical occurrence of *Iuniam*
in Rom 16:7[19]—clearly signifying its feminine status. Therefore,
although we cannot be certain about the Middle Ages and much
of the later period, in more recent times the Latin accusative

Iuniam has been taken as the normally expected feminine accusative and no longer as the exceptional masculine form.

To return to the historical résumé, Brooten also referred to Martin Luther, who, she said, relied heavily on LeFèvre d'Étaples's commentary, and Luther's widely influential and long-standing translation of the Bible first appeared (without his name) in 1522 as *Das Neue Testament deutzsch*, followed by the complete Bible in 1534, and (like LeFèvre) in Rom 16:7 where Ἰουνίαν occurs it reads "Grüsset *den* Andronicum und *den* Juniam" (both with masculine articles), but in Rom 16:15 "Grüsset Philologum und *die* Juliam" (the latter with a feminine article). In addition, *Luther's Works* includes the following: "Andronicus and Junias were famous apostles"[20] and "Greet Andronicus, the manly one, and Junias, of the Junian family, who are men of note among the apostles."[21]

The influence of Luther's Bible cannot easily be overestimated when it is recognized that it was "a literary event of the first magnitude, for it was the first work of art in German prose" and that "the Bible first became a real part of the literary heritage of the German people with Luther."[22] Given this historic framework, Luise Schottroff was direct about Luther's influence with respect to Rom 16:7: "Only since the Middle Ages, and primarily because of Luther's translation, has the view prevailed that Junia was not a woman but a man by the name of Junias."[23]

To cite a final, somewhat random example, the English philosopher John Locke (1632–1704), whose *A Paraphrase and Notes on the Epistles of St Paul*[24] was published posthumously in 1705–1707, affords an opportunity to see how the Junia/Junias matter was addressed by a prominent intellectual in the first few years of the eighteenth century (when the *Paraphrase* was written). Locke, in composing the work, had consulted Isaac Newton and Jean Le Clerc and had studied the works of John Lightfoot, Theodore Beza, and Richard Simon, among many others.[25] Locke's text of Rom 16:7 read as follows: "Salute Andronicus and Junia my kinsmen and my fellow-prisoners, who are of note among the apostles, who also were in Christ before me," while his "paraphrase"—hardly worth the name at this point—contained only two minor changes from his text and, of course, retains "Junia" (and, by the way, "Julia" in Rom 16:15).[26]

Obviously, this exploration of Junia/Junias in New Testament scholarship since the late Middle Ages and into the post-Reformation period could be carried much further, but—with exceptions such as Erasmus and Locke—the reading "Junias" (rather than the more natural "Junia"), whether in Greek, Latin, German, or English and with no overt explanation or justification, continued to take hold and then, when the contracted-name hypothesis appeared, accelerated. To be sure, Johannes Drusius in 1698 "patiently tried to remind his colleagues that *Junia* was the feminine counterpart of *Junius*, just as *Prisca* was of *Priscus*, and *Julia* was of *Julius*."[27] As for the contracted-name theory, which I shall treat in its modern dress momentarily, it was abroad in the mid-eighteenth century when Christian Wilhelm Bose countered it in his 1742 Leipzig doctoral dissertation and doubted that Junia/Junias was a shortened form at all.[28] More recently, Peter Arzt traced a reference to the contracted-name theory back to Richard Bentley around 1720, who, in turn, referred to the Dutch classical philologist, Janus Gruytère (1560–1627),[29] though its influence on Greek New Testaments, with perhaps only one exception, cannot be documented prior to 1927, yet it appears in standard reference works beginning in the fourth quarter of the nineteenth century (see below).

In summary, the feminine understanding of Ἰουνιαν appears to have been dominant for at least the first millennium of Christianity, but then evolved, through what very much appears to have been an arbitrary change from "Junia" to "Junias," into a view that came to be widely assumed/accepted without discussion or justification until the abbreviated-name explanation was invoked. Of course, as we have noticed, when the name appears in the form Ἰουνίαν—which is the only accented form in which it occurs in any New Testament manuscripts—we cannot guarantee that it was taken to be feminine inasmuch as some interpreters simply decided that the name had to be masculine and made it into the nominative Ἰουνίας rather than the natural Ἰουνία. Among the most explicit instances was the Revised Standard Version (RSV) of 1946, which described "Andronicus and Junias" as "men of note among the apostles."[30]

THE CONTRACTED-NAME THEORY

THE SECOND EDITION of the UBS *Textual Commentary* (1994) is undoubtedly the most recent broadly distributed work to repeat the often-repeated proposal that Ἰουνιαν might be understood as Ἰουνιᾶς (masculine) on the grounds that the latter (Junias) might represent the Greek shortened form (called a hypocorism) of a longer masculine name, that is, the Latin *Iunianus*.[1] To be precise, the *Textual Commentary*, after reporting that "some members" of the UBS editorial committee adopted this view, adduced as evidence the 1988 edition of Bauer's *Wörterbuch*, which defined the masculine Ἰουνιᾶς as follows:

> *Junias* (not found elsewh[ere], prob[ably] short form of the common Junianus; cf. Bl.-D. §125, 2; Rob. 172).[2]

The further reference provided by Bauer to Blass-Debrunner, however, was not as unqualified as Bauer's work implied: Blass-Debrunner-Funk (to quote the English version) said:

> Ἰουνιᾶς (= *Junianus?*), if ... Ἰουνιαν R[om] 16:7 means a man (the ancients understood a married couple like Aquila and Priscilla ...).[3]

Yet the Blass-Debrunner *Grammatik* obviously favored the masculine.

It is only fair at this point to acknowledge that Bauer inherited his Ἰουνιᾶς entry from Erwin Preuschen's *Handwörterbuch* (1910[1]),[4] for Bauer (after Preuschen's death in 1920) assumed the editorship of that lexicon and published its second edition (i.e., Bauer's first edition) in 1928. Bauer expanded Preuschen's entry but retained the same references; for example, on the possibility of "Junias" stemming from "Junianus," Preuschen referred to Blass, and against the feminine form of the name, he referred to Lietzmann. If we move back to Friedrich Blass's 1896 *Grammatik des Neutestamentlichen Griechisch* (using H. St. John Thackeray's 1898 translation), he said that in the 'Ιουνίαν of Rom 16:7 "is commonly found a man's name 'Ιουνιᾶς (= Junianus?)."[5] So, the contracted-name explanation was current in 1896. Yet, this theory can be found already in J. H. Thayer's 1886/1889 revision of K. L. W. Grimm's 1862 *Lexicon Graeco-Latinum in libros Novi Testamenti*,[6] though it was not in Grimm; again Thayer enters the name as 'Ιουνίας, but explains it as 'Ιουνιᾶς, "as contr[acted] fr[om] Junianus." Thayer, however, adds that the AV (= KJV) has "Junia," "(a woman's name) which is possible."[7] So the shortened-name view was in circulation by 1886 and Thayer did not obtain it from Blass. Moreover, the theory was adduced even earlier by J. B. Lightfoot in 1871 (as quoted above), by Henry Alford in 1852 in his *Greek New Testament* (see the discussion accompanying Tables 1 and 2), and already in the eighteenth century, a period of less critical scholarship, by Bose (as noted earlier), though it is difficult to know how to trace the theory's ancestry or descent and whether it would be fruitful to do so; we need, rather, to assess the view itself.

What about this commonly repeated hypothesis of a contracted name? Certainly it is common enough, cited in numerous New Testament reference works with approval or as probable (as just illustrated),[8] but what are its merits? Nearly all commentaries, grammars, and most articles on Junia/Junias, if they take any account of the shortened-name explanation, merely nibble around the edges of this theory and provide anything but a thorough analysis. To date, as far as I have discovered, only Richard Cervin (1994) and John Thorley (1996) have tackled the issue head-on.[9] Cervin began by noting what too often has been overlooked—that "Junia" (or better) *Iunia* is a Latin, not a Greek name, and, after consulting the standard dictionaries of Greco-Roman names, past and present, he was satisfied that *Iunias* as a masculine name "does not occur in any extant Greek or Latin document of the NT milieu," and so, "if *Iunias* is indeed a shortened form of the common name *Iunianus*, why then does the name *Iunias* never occur?"[10] Thus, there was no evidence that the specific name *Iunianus* was ever shortened, regardless of what may have happened to analogous names. Then Cervin made his second argument:

Latin masculine names ending in *-us* are rendered as
Greek names in -oς. . . . Latin masculine names in *-o* are
rendered as Greek names in -ων. . . . Latin feminine names
in *-a* are rendered as Greek names in -α or -η . . . ; but
Latin *masculine* names in *-a* are rendered as Greek names
in -aς. . . . What is important for this paper is the fact that
all of the Latin *nomina* ending in *-ius* are regularly transcribed into Greek as names in -ιoς . . . ; likewise the feminine forms of the *nomina* (*-ia*) are rendered into Greek as
names in –ία. . . .

Thus, according to the standard method of transcrib-
ing Latin names into Greek, the *nomen Iunius/Iunia* is rendered as Ἰούνιoς/Ἰουνία. The accusative form (which is
the necessary form in Romans 16) of this name in Latin is
Iunium/Iuniam and the gender is readily discernible. Similarly with the accusative form in Greek, Ἰούνιον/Ἰουνίαν,
where there is again no ambiguity in the form of the
gender.[11]

Cervin's conclusion, then, was that the theory is groundless that
views *Iunias* as the correct name in Rom 16:7 and, further, so
are claims that it is a shortened form of the masculine name
Iunianus.[12]

Thorley began his analysis by asking whether Ἰουνίαν
(so accented) could be masculine, a question raised earlier in
our discussion but left unresolved—if only to await Thorley's
more pointed technical argument. The issue is relevant (as
Thorley pointed out and as treated earlier in my discussion
of the Middle Ages and the Reformation period) (a) because
"Junias" (masculine) occurred in the English RV New Testament of 1881, presumably a translation of Ἰουνίαν, which was
the reading of the Oxford Greek text of the same year that purportedly provided the Greek basis for the RV, and (b) because
J. B. Lightfoot, in his 1871 volume prepared in view of the RV,
stated that "it seems probable that we should render the name
Ἰουνίαν . . . (Rom. xvi.7) by Junias (*i.e.* Junianus), not Junia."[13]
But Thorley showed that of the twenty-six masculine names
in the Greek New Testament that end in unaccented -aς, only
two stem from Latin names: Ἀγρίππας (from Latin Agrippa)
and Ἀκύλας (from Latin Aquila), both of which are from a

common group of Roman *cognomina* of the first declension. Then he added:

> But there is no known cognomen of the form Iunia, nor is such a form ever likely to have arisen when Iunius was such a common "nomen." So it seems Ἰουνίαν cannot be a male name.[14]

What about Ἰουνιᾶς as a name and, specifically, as a contracted name? Thorley proceeded to scrutinize it as follows:

> Is the implied nominative form Ἰουνιᾶς possible? The ending –ᾶς is certainly common enough throughout hellenistic Greek to indicate shortened masculine names (hypocoristics). There are 25 names of this sort in the Greek New Testament. The ending is added not just to Greek names of this sort but also to names of Latin and Semitic origin. . . . However, there are two objections to the form Ἰουνιᾶς.[15]

His first objection is sufficient for our purposes:

> In forming hypocoristics the ending –ᾶς is added to a *consonant*, and when there is a final -ι in the stem of the shortened name[16] this is omitted, whether it is accented . . . or unaccented. . . . From a form such as Junianus (the supposed origin of Ἰουνιᾶς) one would therefore expect Ἰουνᾶς, not Ἰουνιᾶς.[17]

Thorley caps his argument by pointing to a case in the Oxyrhynchus papyri (III. 502, line 6) where the very similar name Ἰουλᾶς occurs, presumably a hypocorism for Julianus (since, as he says, "there is certainly no Latin name Julanus").[18]

Thorley's article is relevant and valuable in one other respect: he surveyed Junia/Junias in several early versions of the New Testament, Old Latin, Vulgate (which has been discussed above), Coptic, and Syriac, and drew the conclusion (quoted more fully at the outset of our discussion) that "there is a strong probability, though not quite a certainty, that the earliest translators took IOYNIAN to be a feminine name."[19]

The clear result of this lengthy discussion of "Junias" (masculine) is that, at least to date, this presumably male name is nowhere attested in the Greco-Roman world. Moreover, with

respect to the accusative singular form Ἰουνίαν in Rom
16:7, "Junias" is nowhere attested either in the form usually
employed, Ἰουνιᾶς—with a masculine accent—or in the for-
merly alleged masculine form, Ἰουνίας, both of which have
been proposed as contracted from the Latin *Iunianus*, and both
of which (as well as the feminine Ἰουνία) would form their
unaccented accusatives as Ἰουνιαν, though only Ἰουνία and
Ἰουνίας would form the accented accusative as Ἰουνίαν.

In addition, as Cervin and Thorley argued, these presumed
Greek masculine forms would not be the result of a contraction
from the Latin *Iunianus*, as so frequently has been proposed for
more than a century by influential New Testament lexicogra-
phers, grammarians, and exegetes; as Peter Lampe stated succinctly, "modern grammars support a masculine reading by
theorizing that 'Junias' was a short form of 'Junianus,' without
being able to quote evidence for this assumption."[20] Already in
1977 Bernadette Brooten, among many recent interpreters, summarized the matter forcibly, but aptly:

> To date not a single Greek or Latin inscription, not a single
> reference in ancient literature has been cited by any of the
> proponents of the *Junias* hypothesis. My own search for an
> attestation has also proved fruitless. This means that we do
> not have a single shred of evidence that the name *Junias*
> ever existed.[21]

That this view is correct is supported by (a) the *continued* lack
of evidence for the existence of the name Junias, and (b) the
difficulties in accrediting it as a contracted name. It is therefore
appropriate and prudent, I think, no longer to place Ἰουνιᾶν
in any New Testament critical edition, either in the text or in
the apparatus, unless it is marked "cj" (for conjecture), nor
should Ἰουνίας be used with reference to Rom 16:7 without
designating this nominative form (and any reference to the accusative form understood as masculine) as a conjecture.

JUNIA/JUNIAS IN CURRENT GREEK NEW TESTAMENTS

I TURN NOW to an examination of accentuation in Junia/Junias as found in our current critical editions of the Greek New Testament; past editions will be important for perspective and will be treated later.

As noted earlier, accents seldom occurred before the seventh century in New Testament manuscripts, though the second correctors (in the sixth, seventh, and ninth centuries, respectively) of two major manuscripts, B of the fourth century and D^{Paul} of the sixth century, accented the word as Ἰουνίαν, as did many later Greek manuscripts, especially from the ninth century and after.[1] Naturally, this means that normal text-critical procedure, which includes heavy reliance on the earliest manuscripts, is not particularly helpful here because of their lack of accents. In spite of this situation—and curiously—the UBS$^{4(1993)}$ listed the support for their reading of Ἰουνιᾶν in the following way:

> Ἰουνιᾶν (*masculine*) (ℵ A B* C D* F G P, *but written without accents*).

Obviously, what is striking is that the only support cited consists of majuscule manuscripts that have no accents, which immediately raises two queries: Are there no accented manuscripts with this masculine form? (to which we already know the answer: none to our knowledge) and, How do the editors know that these manuscripts had the masculine in mind? Nonetheless, when one proceeds to ask how certain the editors were that the text had this masculine form—even when no accents were present in the witnesses cited—one discovers that the reading was assigned an {A} rating: "The letter A indicates that the text is certain"![2] This {A} rating is assigned specifically to the accented form, "'Ιουνιᾶν *(masculine)*," not only in the UBS[4(1993)] text volume but also to 'Ιουνιᾶν (again, accented as masculine) in the first edition of the UBS *Textual Commentary* (1972) without further comment.[3] However, the second edition of the *Textual Commentary* (1994), while retaining the {A} rating, presented a discussion (quoted more fully later on) of the relative merits of the feminine and masculine forms, followed by a disclaimer:

> The "A" decision of the Committee must be understood as applicable only as to the spelling of the name 'Ιουνιαν, not the masculine accentuation.[4]

This, of course, represents a revision of the Committee's earlier decision, though only toward a more neutral position. To return to the UBS[4(1993)] apparatus, it goes on to list the support for the feminine reading as follows:

> 'Ιουνίαν *(feminine)* B[2] D[2] Ψ[vid] 0150 33 81 104 256 263 365 424 436 459 1175 1241 1319 1573 1739 1852 1881 1912 1962 2127 2200 *Byz* [L] *Lect* Chrysostom [to which cop[sa] now should be added][5]

The majuscule Ψ is dated ninth or tenth century, while 0150 and the twenty minuscules listed here date from the ninth to the fourteenth centuries. In addition, the variant 'Ιουλίαν, "Julia," is recorded, supported by 𝔓[46] 6 it[ar, b] vg[mss] cop[bo] eth Jerome,[6] but doubtless influenced by the 'Ιουλίαν of Rom 16:15. Yet it should be noted that the presence of a second feminine variant at this point in Rom 16:7, regardless of its origin, may well be confirmatory of a feminine (rather than a masculine) name in the textual tradition of v. 7.

When Rom 16:7 is consulted in N-A[27(1993)], the text, since it is identical with that of UBS[4(1993)], also reads 'Ιουνιᾶν (masculine), and the apparatus, after listing the major witnesses supporting 'Ιουνίαν, offers the information—and apparently it is only for information—that the majuscules ℵ A B* C D* F G P are *sine acc[entu]* (without accent) and therefore not factors in the text-critical decision.[7] This also was a step forward, and it turns out that this treatment of the unaccented manuscripts was a perfect transition to (and perhaps prophetic of) what happened next. When, in 1998, both the "Jubilee Edition" of Nestle-Aland[27] (containing the fifth corrected printing of N-A[27]) and the third printing of UBS⁴ appeared, the text of Rom 16:7 was altered (correctly and wisely, in our view) to read 'Ιουνίαν, but surprisingly the eight unaccented majuscules (cited earlier as supporting with certainty, in UBS⁴⁽¹⁹⁹³⁾, the clearly masculine reading of the text) are now listed in support of this 'Ιουνίαν reading (!), which has been promoted from the apparatus to the text itself. If this listing was intended to indicate textual support,⁸ it is as misleading as the earlier listing of these unaccented majuscules in UBS⁴⁽¹⁹⁹³⁾ as supporting 'Ιουνιᾶν, the clearly masculine reading.

Moreover, in the 1998 Jubilee N-A²⁷ and the 1998 printing of UBS⁴, where 'Ιουνίαν properly but inexplicably appeared in the text, the clearly masculine form 'Ιουνιᾶν is not even in the apparatus, quite the contrary of what normally happens when a critical edition undergoes a change in its text: one reading moves up to the text as another moves down to the apparatus. In this case, however, suddenly the emperor has no clothes! Apparently this masculine form 'Ιουνιᾶν, once it had been decided that the text was 'Ιουνίαν, disappears altogether from the textual scene! Of course, it should disappear, even though, as we shall discover in a moment, the clearly masculine form had been a Nestle fixture for three-quarters of a century and a UBS constant since the first edition in 1966. Yet in a flash it is gone, and neither the Jubilee Edition nor the 1998 UBS contains a list of changes made in its text as it moved through several printings between the 1993 and the 1998 volumes of N-A²⁷ and UBS⁴, nor is the reason for the change otherwise transparent.⁹

One astounding fact (and disturbing, if one thinks about its implications) requires emphasis again about the UBS and the Nestle-Aland editions: to the best of my knowledge, *never* was the definitely masculine form of 'Ιουνιαν (namely 'Ιουνιᾶν), either when it was designated as the text or after it had been replaced in the text by the 'Ιουνίαν reading, accompanied by any supporting manuscript or other evidence (except when UBS⁴⁽¹⁹⁹³⁾ listed the support of eight early *unaccented* majuscules, which of course were impotent for determining accentuation). In fact, for the greater part of four centuries, as far as I can determine, no apparatus in a Greek New Testament cited 'Ιουνιᾶν as a variant reading to the 'Ιουνίαν in the text—not until Weymouth in 1892 (who cites it in Alford's text—though neither in Alford nor

Weymouth is any manuscript attestation provided)—and never again after that. The reason, as we now know, is simple enough: no such accented form was to be found in any manuscript or anywhere else. Moreover, when Ἰουνιᾶν was interpolated into the New Testament text and became a regular feature of the post-1927 Nestle and Nestle-Aland editions and of all the UBS editions until 1998, no viable manuscript support could be garnered, for there was none.

During this last discussion I have avoided the direct question, "Did the change from Ἰουνιᾶν to Ἰουνίαν in the Nestle-Aland Jubilee Edition (and succeeding printings) and in the UBS printing of 1998 . . . represent a change from masculine to feminine, or does Ἰουνίαν there represent Ἰουνίας, the old, alternate masculine form?" Or is the change purposefully left ambiguous? In contrast to the UBS[4(1993)] apparatus, which identified Ἰουνιᾶν as masculine and Ἰουνίαν as feminine, neither N-A[27(1998)] nor UBS[4(1998)] did that, undoubtedly because Ἰουνιᾶν has disappeared both from the text and the apparatus. However, since the editorial committees of UBS[4] and N-A[27] are identical, it would be natural to assume, if Ἰουνιᾶν is clearly identified as masculine and Ἰουνίαν as feminine in UBS[4(1993)], that the same identifications should apply to N-A[27], whether in the 1993 edition or the 1998, and to UBS[4(1998)].

If we are permitted to make these differentiated and logical identifications of the two forms of Ἰουνιαν, then something more dramatic has occurred in N-A[27] and UBS[4] between their 1993 issues and their corrected versions in 1998—an about-face in which the seven-decade reign of the masculine "Junias" in the Erwin Nestle and Nestle-Aland editions has ended abruptly and almost without notice, to be replaced by the feminine "Junia." This change, of course, also becomes a strong confirmation of the impropriety in permitting the masculine to stand in the text for so long. This is the present state of the Junia/Junias variants in the very latest editions of our standard critical Greek New Testament. A consideration of the past will help us to appreciate the journey we have taken.

JUNIA/JUNIAS IN PAST EDITIONS OF NESTLE, NESTLE-ALAND, AND UBS

IN THE LIGHT of the present situation, some explanation for past exegetical views on Junia/Junias may be found by examining older Nestle and Nestle-Aland editions and also earlier UBS editions. As we have just noted, the Nestle thirteenth edition of 1927 to the Nestle-Aland twenty-seventh edition of 1993 provided no evidence in the apparatus to support the clearly masculine reading ('Ιουνιᾶν) in the text—because there was (and is) none. As for the 'Ιουνίαν form, its existence was not acknowledged in the apparatus of Erwin Nestle's significant thirteenth edition of 1927,[1] but at least from the sixteenth edition of 1936[2] through the twenty-fifth of 1963 it was noted in the apparatus, though only by listing certain editions as witnesses, namely, "HTW" (i.e., Westcott-Hort, Tischendorf, and Weiss), and with no manuscript evidence. In N-A[26] (1979–1991), however, even this reference to supporting editions disappeared, and the apparatus therefore contained no acknowledgment of the undoubtedly feminine 'Ιουνίαν reading. Thus, the masculine 'Ιουνιᾶν that remained in the text until 1998 no longer had any acknowledged rival (except, of course, the 'Ιουλίαν ["Julia"] variant, which virtually all editions report, often [as noted earlier] with a reference to Rom 16:15 as its likely source [e.g., Tischendorf[8], UBS[1,2,3], and the *Textual Commentary*[1,2]]).

Looking back in a similar fashion, it is instructive to examine the UBS[1,2,3] editions, which all had the masculine 'Ιουνιᾶν in the text and which all had identical material in their apparatuses. What was presented there was as misleading as it is astounding. The entry shows the {A} rating for the text, then lists supporting witnesses for Ἰουνιᾶν (masculine). Those witnesses occupy more than two lines, including the familiar eight unaccented majuscules (with no mention of correctors or their corrections), twenty-two minuscules, and *Byz Lect* it[d, dem, e, f, g] vg syr[p, h] cop[sa] arm. Just how misleading was this? The eight majuscules, as already noted, in reality could only attest the letters of the name, not the accent (though the implication is that they support the masculine accent), and the separately listed minuscules (to the extent that they contain accents) actually must have the Ἰουνίαν form; this is patently the case for the nine minuscules that are later found in the list of witnesses in UBS[4](1993) as *supporting the explicitly "feminine" form*! Also, the *groups* of witnesses listed, i.e., the Byzantine text-type minuscules (*Byz*) and the majority of lectionaries (*Lect*), must have "Junia," for they too are listed later in UBS[4(1993)] as attesting the "feminine."[3]

Actually, frustration abounds when one attempts to clarify this situation from comments by various contributors on the Junia/Junias matter. For example, in 1991 the Münster Institut published its massive and valuable data on Romans,[4] which listed 586 manuscripts (fifteen majuscules and 571 minuscules) that have Ἰουνιαν at Rom 16:7 (over against five manuscripts with Ἰουλίαν), but—and here lies the frustration—there is no indication as to which of these hundreds of minuscules were accented or what accentuation was present in any case. Further frustration arises in connection with some exegetical discussions of the matter, four of which are interrelated and presented here as an example: In 1985, Peter Lampe reported a dilemma, namely: "Ἰουνίαν is not attested in the manuscripts of Rom 16:7 and Ἰουνιᾶν is not elsewhere verified as an ancient shortened name."[5] Then, in 1993, Joseph Fitzmyer published his magisterial commentary on Romans, with its otherwise excellent discussion of 16:7, but in which he stated: "Ninth-century minuscule MSS, fitted with accents, already bear the masc. form *Iouniân*, and never the fem. form *Iounían* (see Lampe, 'Iunia/Iunias')."[6] Somewhat before this, in 1991 and 1992, but obviously not in time for use by Fitzmyer, Lampe had published two other articles, in which his earlier dilemma remained but his position had changed:

According to Aland's textual critical apparatus [that would be N-A²⁶], the feminine "Junia" does not appear in the manuscripts. Indeed, most of the medieval scribes of minuscules made Junias a man. But not all, as I discovered recently: Minuscule 33 (9th century) reads the feminine *iounian*. Which reading is to be preferred? Clearly "Junia."[7]

Lampe's second article, a dictionary entry entitled, "Junias… [Gk *Iounia*]" [*sic*] was much the same; it spoke of the Church Fathers of late antiquity who "without exception" identified Andronicus's partner in Rom 16:7 as a woman "as did minuscule 33." "Only later," he continues, "medieval copyists of Rom 16:7 could not imagine a woman being an apostle and wrote the masculine name 'Junias.' This latter name did not exist in antiquity."[8] What is of interest (and what may exonerate both scholars) is that, while both Fitzmyer and Lampe favored the feminine reading, the text (and apparatuses) available to them at the time would have been N-A²⁶ (1979–1991) and UBS³ (1975–1983), but not yet the 1993 N-A²⁷ and UBS⁴, and that may have made all the difference, for two reasons. First, while the apparatus of N-A²⁵ (1963) had noted the existence of the Ἰουνίαν form (but only by referring to three editions that had it in their texts), yet the apparatus of N-A²⁶ (1979–1991) had dropped all mention of that form of Ἰουνιαν but, at the same time, did not provide any manuscript evidence for the masculine form (Ἰουνιᾶν) that stood in its text. Second, on the other hand, the apparatus of UBS³ still retained the forty-two witnesses allegedly attesting the masculine form, Ἰουνιᾶν, including the eight unaccented majuscules! Nor had the second edition of the UBS *Textual Commentary* (1994) yet appeared (see below). Hence, Lampe, followed by Fitzmyer, could say what they did: "Junia" was not attested by manuscripts (à la N-A²⁶), but "Junias" was written in the minuscules (à la UBS³), and any exegete employing N-A²⁶ and UBS³ when those were the latest editions would have come to the very same conclusion that Lampe and Fitzmyer did (though it would be presumptuous to assert that this is how it happened); Lampe obviously had consulted minuscule 33 prior to his second and third articles. It might be noted, incidentally, that C. E. B. Cranfield, in his 1979 commentary on Romans, already had offered an explicit correction of the accent in the Nestle text—it should refer to a "woman" and therefore should be Ἰουνίαν, he asserted,[9] but this timely correction from a major commentary was not to be effected until nearly twenty years later.

In summary, regarding the Ἰουνιαν reading in critical editions of the Greek New Testament that have been standard for many decades, the Erwin Nestle [but not the earlier Eberhard Nestle][10] editions from 1927[13] through 1952[21], all Nestle-Aland editions from 1956[22] through 1993[27], and all four editions of UBS (1966, 1968, 1975–1983, 1993) offered Ἰουνιᾶς (masculine), "Junias," as the text. This long and prevailing chain extending over nearly three-quarters of a century was broken only in the reissue of N-A[27] in 1998 as a special Jubilee Edition in honor of the Nestle and Nestle-Aland editions and their editors and in the 1998 printing of UBS[4], where (as we have observed), without explanation, Ἰουνίαν appeared as the text, which—based on my lengthy discussions—I may now be permitted to interpret with confidence as feminine, that is, "Junia." Regardless of how it came about, this was an admirable and even courageous decision, following, as it did, the extended, indeed the overwhelming dominance of "Junias" in these popular critical editions. But above all, it was a necessary decision in view of the rising waves of both evidence and sentiment during the past few decades for restoring the pristine understanding of Ἰουνιαν as "Junia." The long-standing prevalence of "Junias" in the Nestle editions and the obvious implications for exegesis that flow from it are topics worth consideration, but I must leave such explorations to others. Rather, I need to examine some further issues, past and present.

8

THE ACCENTUATION OF Ἰουνιαν
IN REFERENCE WORKS—AND THE
ATTENDANT CULTURAL BIAS

THE UBS COMMITTEE'S *Textual Commentary* (first edition, 1972) contained no reference to or discussion of the Ἰουνιαν reading, but referred only to the Ἰουλίαν (Julia) variant. Incidentally, since all UBS editions (until 1998) read Ἰουνιᾶς (masculine), it is not surprising that the dictionary published in 1971 in conjunction with UBS had an entry specifying Rom 16:7 only for Ἰουνιᾶς (masculine). To be sure, there was also a dictionary entry for Ἰουνία (specifically "Junia," feminine), but only with reference to a textual variant to Ἰουλία in Rom 16:15, where a few manuscripts read Ἰουνίαν, the same accusative form found in Rom 16:7. There is not, however, even a cross-reference to the possibility of reading it as feminine, "Junia," in 16:7![1] Nor is there any suggestion that this Junia variant to Rom 16:5 should be read as Junias—a masculine—as the dictionary dictates for 16:7! Precisely the same was the *Greek-English Lexicon of the New Testament Based on Semantic Domains*, edited by Johannes P. Louw and Eugene A. Nida.[2] The situation differed a bit for the second edition of the *Shorter Lexicon of the Greek New Testament*, by F. Wilbur Gingrich and Frederick W. Danker,[3] which used the common text of N-A[26] and UBS[3] and which, to be sure, had only the masculine entry for Rom 16:7, "*Junias*," but it added: "unless a woman's name Ἰουνία *Junia* is to be read."

However, in contrast to the first edition (1972), the second edition of the Bruce Metzger's *Textual Commentary* to UBS (1994), summarized the editors' subsequent consideration of the Ἰουνιαν variant and reported that they were now "divided as to how the latter should be accented":

> Some members, considering it unlikely that a woman would be among those styled "apostles," understood the name to be masculine Ἰουνιᾶν ("Junias"), thought to be a shortened form of Junianus (see Bauer-Aland, *Wörterbuch*, pp. 770f.). Others, however, were impressed by the facts that (1) the female Latin name Junia occurs more than 250 times in Greek and Latin inscriptions found in Rome alone, whereas the male name Junias is unattested anywhere, and (2) when Greek manuscripts began to be accented, scribes wrote the feminine Ἰουνίαν ("Junia").[4]

This paragraph exposes the major issues and options concerning the two possible readings, most of which were treated above, with another to be considered now. What is noteworthy in this quotation is the clear exposure of and acknowledgment that an extraneous and prejudicial factor was at work among some in the Committee and that it was operative in a text-critical decision, namely, the assumed "given" that a woman would or could not likely be designated an apostle. Nowhere among the numerous criteria or arguments employed in the discipline of textual criticism over almost two millennia is such a decision-making principle to be found! A more generous interpretation, however, might suggest that the Committee deserves commendation for their candor in reporting such a motivation.

That some biased members among the Committee were said to have seized upon the masculine because "Junias" could be taken as a shortened form for "Junianus" has been analyzed above, but the citation of Walter Bauer's work in that connection prompts a further line of inquiry. Modern reference works to the New Testament have contributed to (or impeded!) the exegetical tradition of Junia/Junias by supporting the view, with a high degree of consistency, that the name in Rom 16:7 was masculine, while, at the same time, discouraging the notion that it was feminine. Prominent in this respect has been Bauer's *Griechisch-deutsches Wörterbuch* (1928²; 1937³; 1952⁴; 1958⁵; its 1988 sixth German edition edited by Kurt and Barbara Aland; and its 1979 second English edition by William F. Arndt, F. Wilbur Gingrich, and Frederick W. Danker), all of which treat the name under the entry, Ἰουνιᾶς, ᾶ, ὁ, i.e., masculine. I have already highlighted the contracted-name portion of the Bauer statement (quoting here the second English edition, though all the German editions have the same explanation), that "Junias" is "not found elsewh[ere], prob[ably] short form of the common "Junianus"; cf. Bl[ass]-D[ebrunner] §125,2; Rob[ertson] 172)," but Bauer's work then goes on, in a curious fashion, to acknowledge that the name might possibly be feminine, but then only to rule it out:

> The possibility, fr[om] a purely lexical point of view, that this is a woman's name, Ἰουνία, ας, *Junia* (M[oulton]-H[oward] [vol. 2, §63] [p.]155; ancient commentators took Andr[onicus] and Junia as a married couple. . .) is prob[ably] ruled out by the context (s[ee] Lietzmann, H[an]db[uch] ad loc).[5]

So now, by following the reference provided by the *Textual Commentary*[2], we have a second motivation for taking Ἰουνιαν as masculine, namely, the context in Rom 16:7. But there is a twofold curiosity here, the first of which involves the rejection of a decision based on "a purely lexical point of view" in favor of the use of the immediate context to determine what a term might signify. Assessing the context (narrow or broad) of a term or idea is, of course, a universally accepted procedure in exegesis (as well as in textual criticism), and that in itself is not faulty or inappropriate; rather, what is unusual here is rejecting the "purely lexical" factor virtually out of hand. One aspect of the lexical factor, of course, is that "Junia" is a regular and indeed very common Latin female name, and Bauer's reference to James H. Moulton and Wilbert F. Howard's 1920 *A Grammar of New Testament Greek* is simply to document the fact that Latin proper names are "very numerous" in the New Testament and that they include "women's names, as *Prisca, Iunia, Drusilla,* and *Iulia.*"[6] The statement of the *Textual Commentary*[2] seventy-four years later that "the female Latin name 'Junia' occurs more than 250 times . . . in Rome alone" brings a portion of these lexical data up to date. A further "lexical" aspect in favor of the feminine form arises from the acknowledgment in Bauer that "Junias," the masculine name, has been found nowhere else—though Bauer (I think) should have said simply "found nowhere" [including Rom 16:7]. With these data in view, rejecting the "purely lexical point of view" is much more serious than might have first appeared.

The second curiosity is how the context of this passage has been used (or not used!) in the decision. Hans Lietzmann's commentary on Romans,[7] which was invoked by Bauer, asserted that Ἰουνιαν "because of the following statements must specify a man [*Mann*]," which, once again, indicated clearly that some other, extraneous hermeneutical principle was operative, for the immediate context of Rom 16:7 (Rom 16:1–16, with 17–27) in no way demanded or even suggested that Ἰουνιαν was male. Actually, quite the contrary is rather easily argued.[8] After all, Romans 16 began with a substantive recommendation of Phoebe (a woman), followed by an extensive list of people to be greeted, both men and women. Twenty-eight individuals were mentioned by name in 16:3–16, and twenty-six of these were sent greetings from Paul (omitting Aristobulus and Narcissus [vv. 10–11], who probably were not Christians, though the Christians in their households were greeted). In addition, two other individuals were greeted, Rufus's mother and Nereus's sister, for a total of twenty-eight, and perhaps twelve of these were known personally by Paul and/or had worked with him. Of the twenty-eight persons who received greetings, seventeen were men and (omitting Junia [v. 7] for the sake of argument) eight were women, but of those described as contributing most through service to the church (again omitting Junia), seven were women and five were men.[9] As many others have noticed, in 16:3 Prisca was listed ahead of Aquila. Also, in 16:6, 12, four of the women were said to have "worked very hard" (κοπιάω), a term Paul used of his own apostolic ministry (1 Cor 4:12; 15:10; Gal 4:11; Phil 2:16) and that of others (1 Cor 16:15–16; 1 Thess 5:12); in 16:3 Prisca (and Aquila) were called Paul's "coworkers" (as were two other women in Phil 4:2–3); and in 16:1 Phoebe was a "deacon" (NRSV; footnote, "minister").[10]

Noteworthy, too, is the fact that five pairs, joined by καί without interrupting descriptions, occurred in the Romans 16 list: first, Prisca *and* Aquila (wife and husband,[11] as indicated in Acts 18; cf. 1 Cor 16:19), then Andronicus *and* Junia, next Tryphaena *and* Tryphosa (both women), then Philologus *and* Julia (man and woman [καί is in the Greek, though not in NRSV]), and immediately thereafter, "Nereus *and* his sister." Certainly this array of five pairs (but we should leave out Andronicus and Junia for the moment), with three out of the remaining four consisting of a male and a female,[12] does not prove that Ἰουνιαν was the female member of that couple, but just as certainly this context does not specify or in any way offer even a hint that Ἰουνιαν was a man, as Lietzmann would have it.

In fact, it would appear that the "argument from context" here is not utilizing the context of the *passage* in question, but the context of the *times*, that is, an interpretive context involving the context of *culture*—the culture of the commentator's time and of the Christian community of that period (for Lietzmann, the early twentieth century). So, the "statements that follow" Ἰουνιαν in Rom 16:7 and which, for Lietzmann, required that a male was intended were the statements that Andronicus and Junia(s) were Paul's fellow prisoners and, specifically, were "outstanding among the apostles." C. E. B. Cranfield's restrained and rather mild comment was: "the assertion of Lietzmann . . . that the possibility of the name's being a woman's name here is ruled out by the context may be dismissed as mere conventional prejudice."[13] What may be more difficult to understand now is that such a sociocultural environment, one imbued with a view of a limited role for women in the church, still could influence some editors of the Greek New Testament in the mid-1990s to the extent that they could impose the masculine form upon an unaccented Greek name (unaccented at least for the first several centuries of Christianity) (a) when all church writers of the first millennium of Christianity took the name as feminine; (b) when there was ample evidence that the name in question was a very common female name at the time of earliest Christianity; and (c) in face of the fact that the alleged masculine forms are nowhere attested in the Greco-Roman milieu.

Views akin to Lietzmann's can be documented time and time again from the period during which Ἰουνιαν was asserted or assumed to be masculine. A. C. Headlam provided a rather balanced treatment of "Junias (or Junia)" in his Hastings *Dictionary of the Bible* article (1899) by stating that if masculine, "Junias" is a shortened form of "Junianus"; if feminine, "Junia" is a common name, but then he added:

> There is little doubt as to whether the two [Andronicus and Junia(s)] are to be included among the apostles—probably they are. . . . In that case it is hardly likely that the name is feminine, although, curiously enough, Chrysostom does not consider the idea of a female apostle impossible.[14]

It is not surprising to discover that Sanday and Headlam's commentary contained virtually the same statement.[15] Much later F. W. Gingrich in *IDB* (1962), where the entry was "Junias," said, "Grammatically it might be feminine (so KJV), though this seems inherently less probable, partly because the person is referred to as an apostle" (ad loc.). In addition, many commentators simply assumed "Junias" to be masculine, without further consideration, such as Bernhard Weiss,[16] T. W. Manson in *Peake's Commentary* (1962),[17] and Ernst Käsemann,[18] to cite a few random examples. Others, such as Otto Michel, summarily dismissed the feminine.[19]

Hence, it is not an idle question to ask what influence such frequently used reference works and commentaries might have had over the years on decisions about the grammatical and text-critical issues involved in the Ἰουνιαν reading of Rom 16:7. In broad terms, it is fair to say that to a large extent our modern lexica, grammars, and many commentaries, especially during the past century, have carried forward—indeed, have aided and abetted—the tradition of "Junias," masculine. In particular, the long-standing dominance of the Bauer lexicon and the Blass-Debrunner grammar both in the Junia/Junias debate and in the shortened-name discussions is as impressive as it is surprising. A striking illustration of such influence is the relatively recent, highly polemical work of Manfred Hauke, who concluded his brief discussion on "A Female 'Apostle Junia'?" with four arguments for the contracted-name view and the masculine form "Junias," *every one* of which is a quotation from or referenced to Blass-Debrunner (with Bauer, and even Lietzmann, mentioned as well)! His fourth argument ("The way that Ἰουνιαν is written is masculine in form. If it were feminine, it would be written as ᾽Ιουνίαν")[20] only reveals how the whole point of the text-critical/grammatical issue was missed, and the statement is best left without comment!

Responses to all such views that evince what I have politely called influence from the context of culture have been strong, and understandably so, especially (though certainly not exclusively) from feminist scholars in North America. An array of poignant statements might be assembled, but permit the following two to represent innumerable others; these are chosen because their wit enhances their poignancy: First, Bernadette Brooten's 1977 formulation regarding Junia has been quoted often by others: "Because a woman could not have been an apostle, the woman who is here called apostle could not have been a woman."[21] Second, Elizabeth Castelli's 1994 analogy has begun to be cited : "The reference to Junia the *apostolos* in 16:7 has inspired remarkable interpretative contortions, resulting ultimately in a sex-change-by-translation."[22]

9

JUNIA/JUNIAS IN GREEK
NEW TESTAMENTS AND THEIR
INFLUENCE ON EXEGESIS

MUCH OF THE discussion to this point has involved the treatment of the Ἰουνιαν reading in present and past critical editions of the Greek New Testament or in standard reference works used in New Testament studies. This is a useful approach, because basic reference works tend to affect the construction of a critical text, readings placed in the text of a critical edition tend to influence exegesis, and exegesis tends to influence the theology and ideology of the church. Yet, as influential as reference works and commentaries might have been and might be, it is the text and the apparatus of various critical editions of the Greek New Testament—but especially of the popular ones—that will have the greatest and most direct influence on exegesis. For this reason, an examination of whether Ἰουνίαν or Ἰουνιᾶν was printed as the text in various Greek New Testaments over the centuries, and whether the alternate reading is registered in the apparatus, will be relevant in our attempt to grasp the "big picture" of this textcritical/exegetical issue. By way of anticipation, the bulk of the Greek New Testaments of the past seventy-five years that are surveyed here have favored the unambiguously masculine Ἰουνιᾶν (Junias)—in sharp contrast to all but one of the earlier editions canvassed, which had Ἰουνίαν (Junia).

Also, since versions of the New Testament often follow a respected critical Greek text then in use (or, in the case of older Roman Catholic translations, a Latin edition) and influence exegesis and theology accordingly, it will be useful to assess how translations treated the Junia/Junias matter, though only English versions will be surveyed here. (It should be a simple matter to assess other modern versions, such as French and German, if that is desired.)[1] First, 'Ιουνιαν in Greek New Testaments (see Table 1, p. 62).

This survey of representative Greek New Testaments from Erasmus through the first quarter of the twentieth century shows virtual unanimity (with one exception) in reading 'Ιουνίαν, presumably the feminine, "Junia." I have to assume that expanding the survey would only extend this consistent pattern.

The following table includes representative Greek New Testaments from the first Nestle edition (1898) to the recent 1998 edition of Nestle-Aland[27]—a hundred years of critical texts—as well as the 1998 printing of UBS[4]. A fourth of the way through this period a significant and almost unanimous change took place in the accentuation of 'Ιουνιαν in these editions—a shift from 'Ιουνίαν to 'Ιουνιᾶν, which continued until the (probably unnoticed) return to 'Ιουνίαν, presumably feminine, in the 1998 N-A[27] and 1998 UBS[4]. (See Table 2, page 63.)

The two tables together show the dramatic change that took place between the Greek New Testaments, on the one hand, from the sixteenth century through the first quarter of the twentieth century, which were one short of unanimity in reading 'Ιουνίαν, and, on the other hand, the Greek Testaments of the last seventy-five years, which almost without exception contained the clearly masculine 'Ιουνιᾶν. I have no explanation for the one exception in the first group, Henry Alford's *Greek Testament* (the Romans volume first appeared in 1852), which was characterized by R. F. Weymouth as having "a leaning toward the "Received Text,"[2] an inclination that should have predisposed him toward 'Ιουνίαν, the reading of the *textus receptus*, but that did not happen; Alford's notes, however, allow that the name "may be fem[inine] ('Ιουνίαν), from 'Ιουνία (Junia) ... or masc[uline], from 'Ιουνιᾶς (Junianus, contr[acted to] Junias)."[3]

As for the second group, after three centuries of 'Ιουνίαν in Greek editions, the unambiguously masculine form appeared in the Erwin Nestle thirteenth edition of 1927, and it occurred in all Greek New Testaments in Table 2 until 1998 (with the exception of the Hodges-Farstad *Majority Text* edition, which, for all practical purposes, was a virtual reproduction of the *textus receptus*

Table 1*

'Ιουνιαν (Romans 16:7) in Greek New Testaments up to the Nestle Editions

Edition	'Ιουνίαν (presumed feminine)	'Ιουνιᾶν (definitely masculine)	Alternate reading in apparatus?
Erasmus (1516)	X		(No apparatus)
Melanchthon (preface, 1545)	X		(No apparatus)
Stephanus (1551) 1576 [apud Hoole, 1674]	X		No
Plantin (1584) 1619	X		(No apparatus)
Elzevir, (1624) 1633 [first "Textus Receptus"]	X		(No apparatus)
Oxford Sheldonian (1675)	X		No
John Gregory (Oxford) (1703)	X		No
Mill (1707) + Mill/Küster, 1710	X		No
Van Maastricht (G.D.T.M.D.) (1711)	X		No
Cyprian (1715)	X		(No apparatus)
Bowyer (1715) 1760	X		(No apparatus)
Wettstein (1751–1752)	X		No
Griesbach (1777) 1796–1806 + 1809	X		No
Knapp (1797) 1829	X		No
Alexander/Isa. Thomas (first American) (1800)	X		(No apparatus)
Schott (1805) 1811	X		No
Pickering (smallest NT) (1828)	X		(No apparatus)
Lloyd (1828) 1873 [TR]	X		(No apparatus)
Lachmann (1831)	X		No
Scholz (1836)	X		No
Tischendorf (1841) 1869-1872[8]	X		No
Alford (1844–1857) + 1888[7]		X	Yes
Buttmann (1856) 1862 + 1898	X		No
Tregelles (1857–1879) 1870	X		No
Scrivener (1859) 1906[4]	X		No
Emphatic Diaglott (Wilson) (1864) 1942	X**		No
Westcott-Hort (1881)	X		Not in notes
Gebhardt (1881) + 1886[3]	X		No
Oxford Greek (behind RV) (1881)	X		No
Critical New Testament (1882)	X		No
Weymouth, Resultant NT (1886) 1905[3]	X		Yes
Baljon (1898)	X		No

Notes to Table 1 appear on page 64.

Table 2*

'Ιουνιαν (Romans 16:7) in Greek New Testaments from Nestle to the Present

Edition	'Ιουνίαν (presumed feminine)	'Ιουνιᾶν (definitely masculine)	Alternate reading in apparatus?
Nestle (Eberhard) (1898[1])	X		No
Nestle (Eberhard) (1899[2])	X		No
Nestle (Eberhard) (1901[3]–1912[9]) 1901[3] + 1906[6]	X		No
British and Foreign Bible Society (1904)	X		?
Souter (1910) + 1947[2]	X		No
von Soden (1913)	X		No
[Eberhard Nestle †1913] Nestle (Erwin) (1914[10]–1923[12]) 1920[11]	X		No
Nestle (Erwin) 1927[13]		X	No
Nestle (Erwin) (1930[14]–1952[21]) 1936[16] + 1941[17] + 1952[21]		X	Yes –ίαν [HTW]
Merk (1933) 1944[5] + 1957[17] + 1984[10] + 1992[11]		X	No
Bover (1943) + 1968[5]		X	No
Nestle-Aland (1956[22]–1963[25]) 1957[23] + 1960[24] + 1963[25]		X	Yes –ίαν [HTW]
Kilpatrick (BFBS[2]) (1958)		X	Yes
Tasker (1964)		X	Yes
UBS (1966[1]) + 1968[2]		X	No
Bover-O'Callaghan (1977)		X	No
[Erwin Nestle †1972] Nestle-Aland (1979[26] [= text of UBS 1975[3]])		X	No
UBS (1975[3])		X	Yes
Nolli (1981)		X	No
Hodges-Farstad (1982) [Majority text = TR]	X		No
Robinson-Pierpont (1991) [unaccented Majority text]	–	–	
Nestle-Aland (1993[27] [= text of UBS 1993[4]])		X	Yes
UBS (1993[4])		X	Yes
[Kurt Aland †1994] Nestle-Aland Jubilee Edition (1998[27-5th rev. printing]) + 2001[27-8th rev. printing]	X		No
UBS (1998[4 -3rd printing]) + 2001[4 -5th printing] [= text of NA 1998, above]	X		No

Note to Table 2 is on page 64.

of the sixteenth century—which had Ἰουνίαν all along). So, there really was no exception from the Nestle 1927[13] text until the dramatic reversal effected in the 1998 Jubilee edition of N-A[27] and in UBS[4] (at the very bottom of Table 2) when the masculine "Junias" was replaced by Ἰουνίαν, presumably the feminine "Junia."[4]

Notes to Table I (page 62)

*For each Greek Testament, the date of the original edition is given in parentheses and also the date of the edition used (if different). If the original edition plus others are cited, they are joined by a + sign, as are multiple editions cited. This list is merely representative, though the most important editions are included to the extent available, plus some older volumes that happen to be in my collection.

**The interlinear English translation, under the Greek Ἰουνίαν, has "Junias."

Note to Table 2 (page 63)

For each Greek Testament, the date of the original edition is given in parentheses and also the date of the edition used (if different). If the original edition plus others are cited, they are joined by a + sign, as are multiple editions cited.

JUNIA/JUNIAS
IN ENGLISH TRANSLATIONS

AN ADDITIONAL TABLE (page 66) provides data that may be instructive, in one way or another, about the relationship between textual criticism and exegesis on the matter of Junia/Junias in Rom 16:7, and that is a table listing numerous English translations of the New Testament and tabulating whether each prints the feminine or masculine form of the name, as well as indicating whether notes to the text furnish the alternate reading (i.e., Junia or Junias as appropriate, but not the Julia variant—which is a separate issue). Since versions generally reflect translators' understandings of critical editions current in their day, whether Greek or (as appropriate) Latin, their translations of Ἰουνιαν also may cast some light on what that name meant to the editors of Greek texts of the New Testament.

The data in Table 3 are not nearly as clean as in the preceding two tables, for the pattern that presents itself on the Junia/Junias matter in English versions moves from a consistent feminine understanding of "Junia" for the first three centuries (1526 to 1833, though the 1833 Dickinson version is an anomaly), then a second, fairly consistent masculine period of about a century (1870s to 1960s, with a few exceptions), followed by nearly three decades (1970 to 1996) of alternation between masculine and feminine, but with an increasing trend of returning to the feminine.

Can we account for any of the alternation between "Junia" and "Junias" in these many English versions? Drawing correlations is difficult, but it might be said that this shift to "Junias" began in earnest with the New Testament of the English Revised Version (RV) that appeared in 1881, along with the ASV in 1901, which were highly esteemed because the RV offered an officially

Table 3*
Junia/Junias (Romans 16:7) in English New Testaments
from Tyndale to the Present

Edition	Feminine (Junia)	Masculine (Junias)	Alternate reading in notes?
Tyndale (1525/1534)	X		(No notes)
Cranmer (1539)	X		(No notes)
"Great Bible," Cromwell (1539)	X		(No notes)
Geneva Bible (1560)	X		(No notes)
Bishops Bible (1568)	X		(No notes)
Rheims (1582) [see 1899 ed. below]	Julia		(No notes)
KJV: = Authorized Version (1611)	X		No

Two centuries intervene here, a period in which the KJV and also the Rheims version were dominant, with reissues and revisions of both. Numerous new translations appeared also.

Edition	Feminine (Junia)	Masculine (Junias)	Alternate reading in notes?
Dickinson, *Productions* (1833) 1837		X	(No notes)
Emphasised Bible (Rotherham) (1872) 1878[2] 1893[12]		X	No
Variorum NT (1876) + 1888	X		Yes
RV: Revised Version (1881)		X	Yes
Rheims: American ed. (1899)** [cf. 1582 above]		X	(No notes)
ASV: American Standard Version (1901) [American revision of RV]		X	Yes
Goodspeed (1902), American Trans. (1923) + 1948		X	No
Complete Bible (Fenton) (1903)		X	No
Weymouth (1903) 1929[5]	X		Yes
Modern Reader's Bible (1907)		X	No
Moffatt (1913) +1922		X	(No notes)
Lamsa (NT, 1940)	X		(No notes)
Ronald Knox (1945)		X	(No notes)
RSV: Revised Standard Version (1946)		X	No
Phillips (1947–1958)		X	(No notes)
Amplified New Testament (1958)		X	(No notes)
NEB: New English Bible (1961)		X	Yes
Noli (1961)		X	(No notes)
NASB: New American Standard Bible (1963)		X	Yes
JB: Jerusalem Bible (1966)		X	No
GNB: Good News Bible = TEV (1966)		X	Yes ("June"!)
NAB: New American Bible (1970)	X		No
LB: Living Bible (1971)		X	No
NIV: New International Version (1973)		X	No
NKJV: New King James Version (1979)	X		No
NJB: New Jerusalem Bible (1985)		X	No
New Century Version (1987)	X		No
New American Bible, revised NT (1987)	X		No
REB: Revised English Bible (1989; rev. of NEB)	X		Yes
NRSV: New Revised Standard Version (1989)	X		Yes
The Message (1993)		X	No
CEV: Contemporary English Version (1995)		X	No
Oxford Inclusive Version (1995)	X		Yes
New Living Translation (1996)	X		Yes

Notes to Table 3 are on page 68.

sanctioned revision of the KJV. The "Junias" of the RV, however, stood in contrast to the "Junia" of the KJV. The year 1881 was also the year when the Westcott-Hort text was issued and quickly thereafter became dominant in Great Britain, but no connection is apparent, although both Westcott-Hort and the Oxford Greek New Testament of 1881, the stated Greek text behind the RV, had the presumably feminine 'Ιουνίαν, while the RV had "Junias." A curious twist, already discussed more than once, accounts for the difference: Joseph Barber Lightfoot's straightforward report that "it seems probable that we should render the name 'Ιουνίαν ... by Junias (*i.e.* Junianus), not Junia."[1] With the feminine presumably in the Greek text of Rom 16:7 for 365 years (with only one exception), what would prompt a committee of eminent scholars to render it as masculine in English? The answer would appear to reside in Lightfoot's context: the two persons in Rom 16:7 were "outstanding among the apostles," so it must be a man, Junias, and this person's maleness could be predicated on the (specious) ground that "Junias" was a shortened name for "Junianus." Hence, the shift that we observe from "Junia" to "Junias" in the RV of 1881 was hardly occasioned by noble, scholarly reasons (if it had been, Lightfoot, the quintessential scholar, might have been expected to have spelled them out).

For whatever reason, this masculine trend became an almost unanimous feature of English versions until 1970, when a zigzag course developed, jutting from masculine to feminine and feminine to masculine until the present time. It remains to be seen whether the combination of the feminine 'Ιουνίαν in the 1998 editions of N-A[27] and UBS[4] and "Junia" in an increasing number of recent English versions will renew the venerable feminine tradition of Rom 16:7 that held sway in the patristic period, in the accented manuscript tradition, and virtually throughout the first four centuries of printed Greek Testaments, and whether such a renewed solidarity will replace the aberrant masculine tradition that infiltrated both our Greek Testaments (for seven decades) and the English New Testament tradition (for some eleven decades). As James Dunn said of 'Ιουνιαν, "The assumption that it must be male is a striking indictment of male presumption regarding the character and structure of earliest Christianity."[2]

Finally, because the change to "Junia" in the two dominant Greek New Testaments has been so recent, I note an apt observation by Ray Schultz, a recently retired Lutheran pastor in Australia, where a 2006 Synodic decision on the ordination of women is pending. He has been a forceful advocate of paying attention to text-critical matters when assessing the portrayal of women in the New Testament and has urged that Junia be properly recognized as an apostle. He warns, however, that few clergy "update their Greek New Testaments," so that "we can expect the promotion of Junias (m[asculine]) for some years to come."[3] This reality will hardly have registered with commentators, much less with textual critics, who themselves will possess and use not only the latest editions of N-A and UBS, but even the latest printings. Are we then faced with another generation of "Junias" while the standard reference works continue their reign and until the now current Greek text (with "Junia") is purchased by students and slowly permeates our theological schools and clergy libraries? How long will it take for translations in English and other languages to follow the new Greek reading? I for one sincerely hope that reference works and translations will be updated in a timely manner (not a likely possibility) and that the United Bible Societies' sales of the current Nestle-Aland and UBS Greek Testaments are brisk!

Notes to Table 3 (page 66)

*For each English version, the date of the original edition is given in parentheses and also the date of the edition consulted (if different). If the original edition plus another are cited, they are joined by a + sign.

**Curiously, this American edition was used for Rheims in *The Precise Parallel New Testament* (New York: Oxford University Press), 1995.

ANDRONICUS AND JUNIA AS "OUTSTANDING AMONG THE APOSTLES"

BY ALL COUNTS, the characterization of Junia, along with Andronicus, as ἐπίσημοι ἐν τοῖς ἀποστόλοις should not have raised any controversy, for the description was widely understood to mean "distinguished among the apostles," rather than being read as "well known to the apostles." Sanday and Headlam in their influential commentary on Romans provided the following reasons for "distinguished among the apostles." First, the translation was in accordance with the literal meaning of ἐπίσημος (stamped, marked), hence: "those of mark among the Apostles." Second, the phrase was thus understood "apparently . . . by all patristic commentators."[1] Over time, however, this phrase, in spite of its clarity in the early centuries of the church, has become a major factor in the debate about whether Junia was, in fact, an apostle, or, alternatively, whether "apostle" really means "Apostle."

One place to begin is to ask what Paul would mean when he uses the term "apostle," a topic often explored. First, it is hardly necessary to remark that the notion of "apostle" was much broader in the earliest church than merely what the arbitrary number "twelve" implies, for it could also designate "messenger," "missionary preacher," or "itinerant missionary."[2] Paul himself, of course, stands outside "the Twelve," as does Barnabas (Acts 14:4, 14; cf. 1 Cor 9:5–6), Apollos (1 Cor 4:6 + 4:9), Epaphroditus (Phil 2:25, but where ἀπόστολος is translated "messenger" in RSV and NRSV), and Silvanus and Timothy (1 Thess 1:1 + 2:7).[3] Second, it is equally clear that Paul, in his letters, feels compelled to defend his apostleship (especially in 2 Cor 12:11–12), which he does vigorously, making it highly unlikely that he would employ the term "apostle" loosely when applying it to others. When Paul defends his apostleship—and thereby defines what apostleship means—he implies that to be an apostle involves encountering the risen Christ (1 Cor 9:1; Gal 1:1, 15–17) and receiving a commission to proclaim the gospel (Rom 1:1–5; 1 Cor 1:1; Gal 1:1, 15–17), and in the process he strongly emphasizes (a) that being an apostle involves "the conscious acceptance and endurance of the labors and sufferings connected with missionary work,"[4] and (b) that apostleship is certified by the results of such toil, namely, "signs and wonders, and mighty works" (1 Cor 15:9–10; 2 Cor 12:11–12). Unless Paul recognized these traits in others, he would not deign to call them "apostles," but Andronicus and Junia obviously met and exceeded his criteria, for—though Paul does not refer to a resurrection experience on their part or describe their labors—they were "in Christ" before he was and, more specific to the point, they were in prison with Paul and therefore had suffered as he had for his apostleship.[5] Ann Graham Brock well phrases the point—though this moves somewhat ahead of our story:

> Thus Junia becomes another[6] example of a woman who was called an "apostle" in early Christian history but whose status has since been mitigated or challenged. Paul's generally sparing use of the term ἀπόστολος indicates his recognition of the term's significance for claiming authority, and therefore his bestowal of the term upon a woman is in turn strong evidence that the category of "apostle" in the early church was not only of considerable importance but also gender inclusive.[7]

Yet, not all scholars have agreed—or will agree—with such a statement, for the history of Junia in New Testament studies makes it clear that once the notion of "apostle" is broached, it is discovered that the description as a prominent apostle and the identification as a woman, for some at least, can no longer coexist.

This disjunction may be illustrated by reference once again to Sanday and Headlam's formulation of the Junia/Junias issue in their influential commentary on Romans, a statement not only typical of the late nineteenth century, but also revealing. After

indicating that "there is some doubt whether this name ['Iou-
νιαν] is masculine, 'Ιουνίας or 'Ιουνιᾶς, a contraction of Junianus, or feminine Junia"—a frequent litany at the time—their
comment continues:

> Junia is of course a common Roman name and in that case
> the two would probably be husband and wife; Junias on
> the other hand is less usual as a man's name. . . . If, as is
> probable, Andronicus and Junias are included among the
> apostles . . . , then it is more probable that the name is mas-
> culine, although Chrysostom does not appear to consider
> the idea of a female apostle impossible."[8]

Then, a few paragraphs later, after quoting Chrysostom's famous
statement about Junia (quoted above), they indicate that Paul's
description of the two is to be read as "outstanding among the
apostles." Next, they go on to affirm that "apostle" in earliest
Christianity had a "wider use" than "the twelve."[9] Here, then,
the issues in Rom 16:7 are clearly exposed, including whether
'Ιουνιαν is female or male (but this has been settled by our preceding discussion). Two intertwined issues remain:
1. Is apostleship restricted by gender?
2. Are the two individuals distinguished apostles, or merely
    well known to the apostles?
Sanday and Headlam had settled the second issue to their
satisfaction: the individuals were "distinguished" apostles, but
by their explicit statement, the identification of 'Ιουνιαν as a
woman would be excluded by the centuries-long understanding
that the two people greeted by Paul were not only apostles, but
prominent ones. So, something had to give, and it was the twelve
centuries of unanimous tradition (and several more nearly
unanimous) that 'Ιουνιαν was Junia. 'Ιουνιαν, therefore, must
become Junias. A similar example from only a decade ago, also
reported earlier, is the 1994 statement in the *Textual Commentary*[2] to UBS that "Some members [of the UBS Committee], considering it unlikely that a woman would be among those styled
'apostles,' understood the name to be masculine."[10] Of course,
this statement represents an improvement over the position
taken in the first edition of 1972, when no question at all was
raised about placing the male Junias in the UBS text.

Hence—in the minds of some—the gender of Ἰουνιαν is intertwined with the interpretation of the phrase describing the two individuals, so that, if the phrase means "distinguished apostles," Ἰουνιαν is a man; or, if a man is designated, the phrase more easily carries the sense of "prominent apostles." On the other hand, if the name is female, the phrase means "of note in the eyes of the apostles," that is, the person is not an apostle, or, if the phrase means "well known to the apostles," a woman is more readily acceptable. Is it mere coincidence that often those who assume the masculine "Junias" find little or no difficulty in opting for "outstanding among the apostles," such as Ernst Käsemann, who assumed Junias without comment and stated that ἐπίσημοι "does not mean merely 'esteemed by the apostles' . . . but 'prominent among them'"?[11]

A recent example has a different coupling of views: an affirmation of Ἰουνιαν as a woman and an extended argument that ἐπίσημοι ἐν τοῖς ἀποστόλοις means "well known to the apostles." I note the juxtaposition of these two interpretations, though I would not presume to judge motives, but it is interesting to observe that, over time, the male "Junias" and the female "Junia" each has his or her alternating "dance partners"—first one, then the other: first and for centuries, Junia with "prominent apostle"; then Junias with "prominent apostle." Then for a time Junia disappears from the scene, hoping upon her return to team up once again with "prominent apostle," only to encounter "known to the apostles" cutting in during this latest "dance."

The recent view is presented by Michael H. Burer and Daniel B. Wallace in "Was Junia Really an Apostle? A Re-examination of Rom 16.7"[12] in one of our most prominent journals. The issue can be stated succinctly, using their terminology: Does the phrase ἐπίσημοι ἐν τοῖς ἀποστόλοις have an *inclusive* or *exclusive* sense? That is, is it *inclusive* in the sense that a person is prominent or distinguished as a member of her or his own group? Or is it *exclusive*, stating that someone is prominent or well known, as an outsider, to members of a group not his or her own?

As noted, the authors accept Ἰουνιαν as feminine, but they do not wish to admit the *inclusive* sense of ἐπίσημοι ἐν τοῖς ἀποστόλοις (that Andronicus and Junia were "outstanding among the apostles" or "prominent as apostles"), but only the *exclusive* sense ("well known to the apostles").[13] Their case is based (a) on a search of *TLG* and other databases and publications of Greek texts and (b) on their subsequent selection of "a few dozen passages" deemed relevant out of the resultant "several hundred pages of text" that contained instances of ἐπί-σημος and its cognates. Considered relevant were constructions of ἐπίσημος with a genitive modifier or with ἐν plus the dative.[14] Among these, a distinction was drawn between "personal" (where the context involved people) and "impersonal" instances.[15] These relatively few remaining passages then were utilized to support their "working hypothesis," namely, that "if in Rom 16.7 Paul meant to say that Andronicus and Junia were outstanding *among* the apostles, we might have expected him to use the genitive (τῶν) ἀποστόλων," but if no comparison were intended, we might expect ἐπίσημος with ἐν + dative.[16] The examples provided number twenty-two (eliminating one lacunose papyrus), but three more if relevant examples in the footnotes are included, for a total of twenty-five. While it is unclear whether more examples were at hand, even a cursory examination of those presented raises significant doubts about the authors' stated thesis—that the phrase describing Andronicus and Junia "is more naturally taken with an exclusive force rather than an inclusive one."[17] Burer and Wallace, however, deserve our gratitude for an essay that offers appropriate cautions and is eminently fair to opposing positions, and we are indebted to them for bringing these data to the scholarly discussion. Yet a number of problems emerge as one examines their evidence.

Three extensive critiques of their work are known to me: my own, which appeared in 2002 in the article that forms the basis for this book; a second by Richard Bauckham,[18] also published in 2002; obviously we worked independently. The third, more recent, is by Linda Belleville in 2005.[19] Generally speaking, "no holds are barred" since the issue is taken seriously by all concerned.

First, Burer and Wallace offered examples from *biblical and patristic Greek*, numbering seven (including two from 1 Maccabees in their footnote 52), two of which are personal and five impersonal. The single personal use of ἐπίσημος + genitive (3 Macc 6:1) is inclusive, and the single personal ἐπίσημος + ἐν + dative (*Pss. Sol.* 2:6) is, they assert, exclusive, fitting the authors' proposed pattern. However, the five impersonal instances are all inclusive, even though three of them (Add Esth 16:22 and 1 Macc 11:37 and 14:48) have ἐν + dative, which is contrary to the alleged pattern. Hence, the authors' conclusion on biblical and patristic Greek usage was overdrawn and misleading in view of the examples provided, for they asserted that "every instance of *personal* inclusiveness used a genitive rather than ἐν" (but there is only one example!) and "every instance of ἐν plus *personal* nouns supported the exclusive view"[20] (but again there is only one instance!). However, this latter single instance (*Pss. Sol.* 2:6), on which Burer and Wallace place considerable emphasis as a close parallel to Rom 16:7, is invalidated for *not being parallel* to Rom 16:7 by Richard Bauckham.[21] So far, this leaves Burer and Wallace's "working hypothesis" somewhat in shambles and with exceptionally minimal data.

Next, Burer and Wallace turned to evidence from the *papyri* and *inscriptions*, offering first three examples from the papyri, all containing ἐπίσημος + genitive, with no instances of ἐν + dative. All were from Oxyrhynchus (P.Oxy. XII:1408; XVI:2108; and XXXIV:2705) and involved *impersonal* constructions, and they were described quite properly as "not terribly strong" parallels.[22] There were four examples from inscriptions, all virtually identical in character; all involve persons; all have the ἐν + dative construction; and, according to the authors, all have the exclusive sense—again fitting their proposed pattern, even though they admitted that "these data are not plentiful." The example treated in detail (TAM II west wall. coll. 2.5) has been provided, however, with a translation that is obviously question-begging: the text refers to a man who is "not only foremost [πρῶτος] in his own country, but also *well known* [ἐπίσημος] to the outside population [ἐν τῷ ἔθνει]."[23] Might this not be translated as "not only foremost in his native town, but prominent among the nation" (i.e., among the nationals)?[24] The authors argued that the strong contrast (οὐ μόνον . . . ἀλλὰ καί) was between an insider and outsiders,[25] making it exclusive (in their terminol-

ogy), but could not the contrast just as well be between a specific locality and a broader area (inclusive)? Though questions
remain, Burer and Wallace viewed the inscriptions as furnishing
four personal ἐν + dative instances that follow their "working
hypothesis," i.e., are exclusive, though the examples include no
genitive constructions at all. Linda Belleville, however, under-
stands all the examples from inscriptions to be inclusive, and, I
think, with good reason.[26]

When the next examples were presented from *classical Greek
literary texts* and *Hellenistic texts*, no improvement in the cogency
or consistency of the evidence was to be observed. From classical literature three examples were given; the first is impersonal
(Lycurgus, *Against Leocrates*, 129), the second personal (Euripides, *Bacchae*, 967), but each has a dative case without ἐν. Burer
and Wallace interpret both as exclusive, though I would question whether the second is so clearly exclusive—when it refers
to Pentheus as ἐπίσημον ὄντα πᾶσιν. Only the third is a solid
example: in Euripides, *Hippolytus* 103, Aphrodite is described
as "prominent/splendid among/to mortals," where the exclusive view is apparent because she is not a mortal.[27] In any event,
the result for classical literature is that there are two personal
instances with the dative (but one without ἐν), and again not a
single example with the genitive.

Finally, the authors offered seven examples from Hellenistic
literature, which were described as "a bit more varied in their
nuances." First came three impersonal instances, in which the
evidence goes both ways—the inclusive view expressed both
by ἐν + dative (in Lucian and in Philo) and by the genitive (in
Galen). Second, there were five personal examples, if we include
one provided in a footnote; three followed the "working hypothesis" of (a) inclusion expressed by the genitive (Lucian, *Peregr.*
6.1; Herodian, 1.7)[28] and (b) exclusion by ἐν + dative (Lucian,
Harmonides 1.17, though without ἐν). Lucian, though, "is not
consistent in this" (as our authors admitted), for in another personal example he employs the ἐν + dative construction *inclu-
sively* in a context in which servants are urged to raise their voices
and to be "prominent/conspicuous among the claque/hired
applauders" (ἐπίσημος ἔσῃ ἐν τοῖς ἐπαινοῦσι—Lucian,

Merc. Cond. [*On Salaried Posts in Great Houses*], 2.8). This case, Burer and Wallace affirmed, represents "the first parallel to Rom 16.7 we have seen that could offer real comfort to inclusivists. It is unmistakable, it is personal, and it is rare."[29] The fifth example, from Josephus (*Jewish War* 2.418), interestingly was yet another ἐπίσημος ἐν + dative instance that is inclusive—contrary to their "working hypothesis." The result is that Hellenistic literature yields five instances involving people, including two cases of ἐπίσημος + genitive that are inclusive and one of ἐπίσημος + ἐν + dative that is exclusive—consistent with the authors' hypothesis—but, strikingly, the other two instances have ἐν + dative *and yet are inclusive*! So the score (so to speak) would be two-to-two between expressing inclusiveness by ἐπίσημος + genitive or by ἐπίσημος + ἐν + dative in this important body of literature. Indeed, the balance might be tipped two-to-three in favor of ἐπίσημος + ἐν + dative if an additional instance, found in their footnote 65 (Lucian, *Peregr.* 22.2) should turn out to be personal. Actually, this reference was a mistake (as Bauckham pointed out),[30] and, fortunately, Linda Belleville was able to locate it: Lucian, *Dialogues of the Dead*, 438; it is both personal and inclusive, and a near perfect parallel to Rom 16:7![31]

> ἐν αὐτοῖς δὲ ἐπίσημοι Ἰσμηνόδωρος . . . ("Most distinguished among whom were Ismenodorus. . . .") (Lucian, *Dialogues of the Dead* 438)

> οἵτινές εἰσιν ἐπίσημοι ἐν τοῖς ἀποστόλοις ("They are most distinguished among the apostles") (Rom 16:7)

Bauckham's and Belleville's rigorous examinations of Burer and Wallace's examples finds them wanting—more so than I had. Bauckham, for instance, finds that their method has "serious defects," providing only a portion of the evidence they claim to have; what they do provide cannot be used for statistical analysis; and "the vagueness about the amount of evidence makes the conclusions drawn from it highly tendentious, even misleading."[32] And Belleville weighs in with two conclusions: In Greek, "primary usage of ἐν and the plural dative (personal or otherwise) inside and outside the NT (with rare exceptions) is *inclusive* "in"/"among" and not *exclusive* "to."[33] and "They fail to offer one clear biblical or extra-biblical Hellenistic example of an 'exclusive' sense of ἐπίσημος and a plural noun to mean 'well known to.'"[34] Rather, from her display of ten such examples, including literary texts and inscriptions, which Burer and Wallace claimed would have the exclusive sense, it is apparent, as she states, that they "bear the inclusive meaning 'a notable member of the larger group.'"[35] Both Bauckham and Belleville found (much as I did) that "of all the examples listed by Burer and Wallace as *exclusive*, only Euripides' *Hippolytus* 103 is truly so," with Bauckham explaining that Euripides, five centuries earlier, "might have been writing at a time when ἐπίσημος had not yet acquired a comparative sense."[36]

In summary, accepting the (occasionally disputable) interpretations of Burer and Wallace as to whether the various instances carry an inclusive or exclusive sense, I found the thirteen personal examples they utilized to come out as follows: (a) eight ἐπίσημος + dative instances (though not all have ἐν) that are exclusive; (b) no ἐπίσημος + genitive that are exclusive; and (c) three ἐπίσημος + genitive that are inclusive; but—contrary to the proposed pattern—(d) two (but now three) personal cases that have ἐπίσημος + ἐν + dative *but are also inclusive*—the construction found in Rom 16:7, again frustrating any effort to trace the "uniform picture"[37] hoped for in the authors' "working hypothesis"; in fact, whether inclusiveness is expressed by ἐπίσημος with the genitive or with ἐν plus the dative is virtually, if not literally, a toss-up on the basis of the evidence presented. Even when the impersonal cases are considered, the tally results in (a) one (but only one) exclusive case with the dative; (b) no exclusive ἐπίσημος + genitive instances; (c) six inclusive instances with the genitive (the "expected" results); but (d) also five ἐν + dative *inclusive* cases.

Of course, these data are extremely minimal overall, but the remarkable fact is that Burer and Wallace, on the basis of the evidence presented, affirmed not only that their "few dozen passages" contained "definite patterns"[38] (which they do not), but that "repeatedly in biblical Greek, patristic Greek, papyri, inscriptions, classical and Hellenistic texts, our working hypothesis was borne out. The genitive personal modifier was consistently used for an inclusive idea, while the (ἐν plus) dative personal adjunct was almost never so used."[39] Actually, this "almost never so used" ἐν + dative is indeed used twice (but now three times) over against the "consistently used" genitive's mere three cases! Moreover, they present no instances of personal ἐπίσημος constructions that are inclusive from the papyri, inscriptions, or classical literature. The data are meager indeed and of necessity raise questions about the validity of claims made on such a basis. Therefore, when Burer and Wallace further conclude that in Rom 16:7 "ἐπίσημοι ἐν τοῖς ἀποστόλοις *almost certainly* means 'well known *to* the apostles,'"[40] their own evidence suggests that such a statement is not without very significant difficulty.

This is supported by the critical evaluations by Bauckham and Belleville, both presenting more detailed critiques than I had, and surely these three evaluations, singly perhaps, but certainly collectively, should put to rest any notion that ἐπίσημοι ἐν τοῖς ἀποστόλοις carried the sense of "well known to/esteemed by the apostles." Again, it is clear that Andronicus and Junia, in Paul's description, were "outstanding apostles."

CONCLUSION:
THERE WAS AN APOSTLE JUNIA

IF THESE GRAMMATICAL and textual examples and our charts and statistics regarding Ἰουνιαν as a woman and Andronicus and Junia as "outstanding apostles" were not to provide a clear-cut solution to the Pauline phrase in Rom 16:7—which, of course, I think they do—there remains another path toward an answer, and it lies near at hand: the statement of Chrysostom quoted at the outset of our Junia investigation. Indeed, it is remarkable to me that Burer and Wallace did not, themselves, ever refer to Chrysostom, much less quote his statement, although Chrysostom's name occurs in two footnotes in material they cited from other scholars.[1] Chrysostom, as we noted earlier, appears early in the apparently unanimous list of writers from the church's first millennium who understood Ἰουνιαν as feminine, a view adopted by virtually all printed Greek New Testaments until the twenty-seventh Nestle edition appeared in 1927—with perhaps a single exception. Certainly "Junia" was also understood by all the English versions of Rom 16:7 up to the 1830s. But, as Burer and Wallace pointed out, the recognition of Junia as a woman is an issue separate from acknowledging that she was an apostle. Indeed, here is where Chrysostom makes his mark, for he leaves no doubt that Junia was an apostle and that ἐπίσημοι ἐν τοῖς ἀποστόλοις is inclusive—in addition, Junia was an outstanding apostle (along with Andronicus):

> Even to be an apostle is great, but also to be prominent among them (ἐν τούτοις ἐπισήμους)—consider how wonderful a song of honor that is. For they were prominent because of their works, because of their successes. Glory be! How great the wisdom of this woman that she was even deemed worthy of the apostle's title.[2]

If someone still objects by asserting that the Greek phrase in Chrysostom meant only "well known to the apostles," that would render the sentence meaningless, namely, "To be an apostle is great, but to be well known to them, what a wonderful song of praise that is." Chrysostom, after all, was clearly moving from the lesser to the greater or (more accurately) from the great to the greater, which surely demands the inclusive force: Chrysostom affirmed that Junia was an apostle and, what is more, a distinguished apostle. Finally in this connection, the reminder a century ago from James Denney is still pertinent today. In commenting on ἐπίσημοι ἐν τοῖς ἀποστόλοις in Rom 16:7, he said:

> It might mean well-known to the apostolic circle, or distinguished as Apostles. The latter sense is that in which it is taken by "all patristic commentators" . . . *whose instinct for what words meant in a case of this kind must have been surer than that of a modern reader.*[3]

Therefore, the conclusion to this investigation is simple and straightforward: *there was an apostle Junia.* For me, this conclusion is indisputable, though it will not, I fear, be undisputed—for the "cultural context" of which I spoke earlier remains in many quarters. Yet, if this perfectly natural reading of Ἰουνιαν in Rom 16:7 as feminine, followed by all early church writers who treated the passage, had continued in late medieval to modern times, lengthy and tedious studies like the present one would be unnecessary, as would the manipulations and machinations of countless male scholars (presumably otherwise enlightened) over the past two centuries. But far more significant and regrettable is the unnecessary alienation of women that has taken place and continues in many quarters of the church, though that situation has roots earlier and broader than the Junia issue, by which the latter also was most certainly influenced.

Manfred Hauke, in (mis)treating Junia in Rom 16:7, views that passage as one of three in the Pauline corpus that exclude women from teaching roles in the church, along with 1 Cor 14:34-35 and 1 Tim 2:8-15. His argument is of interest:

> Even assuming that "Junia" could be interpreted as feminine, the function of a "lady apostle" need not lie in the

area of public preaching. The strict "ban on teaching" in 1 Corinthians 14 and 1 Timothy 2 would not be easy to understand given the supposed existence of a female missionary preacher.[4]

But this mode of argumentation is significantly weakened once it is clear that a woman, Junia, is referred to as an apostle in Rom 16:7 and that 1 Cor 14:34-35 is likely a non-Pauline interpolation into Paul's letter (as discussed earlier). Then it is no longer Rom 16:7 that is out of place in this threesome of passages, but 1 Tim 2:8-15, which, from the customary critical standpoint, is the composition of a later Paulinist, one of whose thrusts is the subordination of women, a trend begun already in the earlier deutero-Pauline letters of Ephesians (5:22-24) and Colossians (3:18). Numerous scholars will accept such decisions regarding the three passages and will declare that the assumed Pauline restriction on teaching in the church by women has disappeared, but how these academic conclusions "play out" in the larger Christian communities is another issue. Yet, even apart from these other passages—and how critical scholarship may view them—it remains a fact that there was a woman apostle, explicitly so named, in the earliest generation of Christianity, and contemporary Christians—lay people and clergy—must (and eventually will) face up to it.

Do textual criticism and exegesis affect one another? Absolutely, but human beings carry out not only textual criticism and interpretation but implementation as well, and that makes all the difference.

ABBREVIATIONS

AB	Anchor Bible (Doubleday)
ABD	*Anchor Bible Dictionary*
ANTF	Arbeiten zur neutestamentlichen Textforschung
ASV	American Standard Version
AV	"Authorized Version" (= KJV)
BAGD	Bauer, Arndt, Gingrich, Danker, *Greek-English Lexicon of the New Testament and Other Early Christian Literature* (2d ed., 1979)
BDAG	Bauer, Arndt, Gingrich, Danker, *Greek-English Lexicon of the New Testament and Other Early Christian Literature* (3d ed., ed. F. W. Danker, 2000)
BDF	Blass, Debrunner, Funk, *A Greek Grammar of the New Testament and Other Early Christian Literature*
BETL	Bibliotheca ephemeridum theologicarum lovaniensium
BFBS	British and Foreign Bible Society
BT	*The Bible Translator*
BTB	*Biblical Theology Bulletin*
BZNW	Beihefte zur *Zeitschrift für die neutestamentliche Wissenschaft*
CBQ	*Catholic Biblical Quarterly*
Ebib	Études bibliques
EDNT	*Exegetical Dictionary of the New Testament*
ExpT	*Expository Times*
fl.	"flourished," a scholar's productive years
HNT	Handbuch zum Neuen Testament
HTR	*Harvard Theological Review*
HTS	Harvard Theological Studies
ICC	International Critical Commentary

IDB	*The Interpreter's Dictionary of the Bible*
ISBE	*International Standard Bible Encyclopedia*
JAC	Jahrbuch für Antike und Christentum
JBL	*Journal of Biblical Literature*
JFSR	*Journal of Feminist Studies in Religion*
JSNT	*Journal for the Study of the New Testament*
KEK	Kritisch-Exegetischer Kommentar über das Neue Testament
KJV	King James Version of the Bible, 1611
N-A	Editions of the Greek New Testament by Eberhard or Erwin Nestle and Kurt Aland
NICNT	New International Commentary on the New Testament
NovT	*Novum Testamentum*
NovTSup	Supplements to Novum Testamentum
NRSV	New Revised Standard Version of the Bible, 1989
NTS	*New Testament Studies*
𝔓	preceding a number, indicates a papyrus manuscript
PG	Jacques Paul Migne, *Patrologia Graeca*, 162 vols.
PHI	*Packard Humanities Institute* [CD-ROM]
PL	Jacques Paul Migne, *Patrologia Latina*, 217 vols.
RSV	Revised Standard Version, 1946
RV	Revised Version of the Bible, 1881
SBL Syms	Society of Biblical Literature Symposium Series
SD	Studies and Documents
SNTSMS	Society for New Testament Studies Monograph Series
TEV	Today's English Version
TJT	*Toronto Journal of Theology*
TLG	*Thesaurus Linguae Graecae* [CD-ROM]
TR	*Textus receptus*, the "received text," the text of the Greek New Testament in printed editions to the latter part of the nineteenth century
UBS	United Bible Societies
WBC	Word Biblical Commentary
ZNW	*Zeitschrift für die neutestamentliche Wissenschaft*

NOTES

Foreword

1. The debate grows ever more complex, but a useful introduction is offered in Karl P. Donfried, ed., *The Romans Debate* (rev. and exp. ed.; Peabody, Mass.: Hendrickson, 1991).

2. Karl P. Donfried, "A Short Note on Romans 16," in *The Romans Debate*, 44–52; Harry Y. Gamble, *The Textual History of the Letter to the Romans: A Study in Textual and Literary Criticism* (Grand Rapids: Eerdmans, 1977), 36–95, esp. 84–95.

3. Peter Lampe, *From Paul to Valentinus: Christians at Rome in the First Two Centuries,* trans. Michael Steinhauser, ed. Marshall D. Johnson (Minneapolis: Fortress Press, 2003), 153–83. The translation is partially revised and updated from the German edition published in 1989.

4. Of special importance is the article of Bernadette Brooten, "'Junia ... Outstanding among the Apostles' (Romans 16:7)," in *Women Priests: A Catholic Commentary on the Vatican Declaration*, ed. L. and A. Swidler (New York: Paulist, 1977), 141–44.

5. See below, p. 32–33, 71, 79–80.

6. See below, p. 40, 55–59; cf. 67.

1. Textual Criticism and Exegesis

1. See my essay "The Multivalence of the Term 'Original Text' in New Testament Textual Criticism," *HTR* 92 (1999) 245–81.

2. Barbara Aland, Kurt Aland, Johannes Karavidopoulos, Carlo M. [Cardinal] Martini, and Bruce M. Metzger, eds., *Novum Testamentum Graece post Eberhard et Erwin Nestle* (27th ed., 8th corrected printing, with Papyri 99–116; Stuttgart: Deutsche Bibelgesellschaft, 2001), known as Nestle-Aland[27]; Barbara Aland, Kurt Aland, Johannes Karavidopoulos, Carlo M. [Cardinal] Martini, and Bruce M. Metzger, eds., *The Greek New Testament* (4th rev. ed., 5th printing, with Papyri 98–116; Stuttgart: Deutsche Bibelgesellschaft/United Bible Societies, 2001), known as UBSGNT[4] or UBS[4]. Both works contain the same Greek text and both were produced in cooperation with the Institute for New Testament Textual Research, Münster.

3. *Proceedings of the British Academy* 27 (1941) 15. The volumes in question are S. C. E. Legg, ed., *Nouum Testamentum graece secundum textum Westcotto-Hortianum: Euangelium secundum Marcum* (Oxford: Clarendon Press, 1935); idem, ed., *Nouum Testamentum graece secundum textum Westcotto-Hortianum: Euangelium secundum Matthaeum* (Oxford: Clarendon Press, 1940).

4. E. J. Epp, *The Theological Tendency of Codex Bezae Cantabrigiensis in Acts* (SNTSMS 3; Cambridge and New York: Cambridge University Press, 1966). See now, idem, "Anti-Judaic Tendencies in the D-Text of Acts: Forty Years of Conversation," in *The Book of Acts as Church History: Text, Textual Traditions and Ancient Interpretations/Apostelgeschichte als Kirchengeschichte: Text, Texttraditionen und antike Auslegungen*, ed. Tobias Nicklas and Michael Tilly (BZNW 120; Berlin and New York: de Gruyter, 2003), 111–46.

5. E. J. Epp, "The New Testament Papyri at Oxyrhynchus in Their Social and Intellectual Context," in *Sayings of Jesus: Canonical and Non-Canonical. Essays in Honour of Tjitze Baarda*, ed. W. L. Petersen, J. S. Vos, and H. J. de Jonge (NovTSup 89; Leiden: Brill, 1997), 47–68; idem, "The Codex and Literacy in Early Christianity and at Oxyrhynchus: Issues Raised by Harry Y. Gamble's *Books and Readers in the Early Church*," *Critical Review of Books in Religion* 11 (1997) 15–37; "The Oxyrhynchus New Testament Papyri: 'Not without Honor Except in Their Hometown'?" *JBL* 123 (2004) 5–55 (Presidential Address, Society of Biblical Literature, 2003).

6. "The Multivalence of the Term 'Original Text.'"

7. Ibid., esp. 276–81.

8. Brooke Foss Westcott and Fenton John Anthony Hort, *The New Testament in the Original Greek* (2 vols.; London: Macmillan, 1881–82; vol. 2, 2d ed., 1896).

9. For an extended discussion, see Epp, "The Multivalence of the Term 'Original Text,'" esp. 264–66, which summarize relevant portions of David C. Parker, *The Living Text of the Gospels* (Cambridge: Cambridge University Press, 1997).

10. Parker, *Living Text of the Gospels*, 209, and his entire chap. 12, "The Living Text," 203–13. Contrast the view of Kurt and Barbara Aland in *The Text of the New Testament: An Introduction to the Critical Editions and to the Theory and Practice of Modern Textual Criticism*, 2d ed. (Grand Rapids: Eerdmans; Leiden: Brill, 1989), 280, who state, as the first of twelve basic text-critical principles, that "only one reading can be original, however many variant readings there may be," though they concede that "very rare instances . . . present an insoluble tie between two or more alternative readings."

11. See Epp, "The Multivalence of the Term 'Original Text,'" 274–77, for a discussion of proposed dimensions of meaning in the term "original text," including the (newly coined) terms "predecessor," "autographic," "canonical," and "interpretive" text-forms.

12. On the latter, see Bart D. Ehrman, *The Orthodox Corruption of Scripture: The Effect of Early Christological Controversies on the Text of the New Testament* (New York: Oxford University Press, 1993).

13. This is the classic issue of the two early textual streams in which the Acts has been transmitted. For one interpretation, see my early work, *The Theological Tendency of Codex Bezae Cantabrigiensis in Acts.* The older view of Friedrich Blass, that Luke wrote two versions of Acts, has been revived in recent times by several scholars; for an excellent assessment of recent and current views, see Joël Delobel, "The Text of Luke-Acts: A Confrontation of Recent Theories," in *The Unity of Luke-Acts,* ed. J. Verheyden (BETL, 142; Leuven: Peeters–University Press, 1999), 83–107.

14. P.Oxy LXVI.4499 (late third/early fourth century). The first full study is by D. C. Parker, "A New Oxyrhynchus Papyrus of Revelation: $\mathfrak{P}^{115}$ (P.Oxy. 4499)," *NTS* 46 (2000) 159–174.

15. In this case not because of the argument that "the shorter reading is preferable" but on the basis of internal evidence, specifically, the passage's theological and literary context in Mark. Indeed, the "shorter reading" argument has fallen under suspicion in recent decades: see a summary of the discussion in E. J. Epp, "Issues in New Testament Textual Criticism: Moving from the Nineteenth to the Twenty-First Century," in *Rethinking New Testament Textual Criticism,* ed. D. A. Black (Grand Rapids: Baker, 2000), 27–30.

16. See Adela Yarbro Collins, "Establishing the Text: Mark 1:1," in *Texts and Contexts: Biblical Texts in Their Textual and Situational Contexts: Essays in Honor of Lars Hartman,* ed. T. Fornberg and D. Hellholm (Oslo, Copenhagen, and Stockholm: Scandinavian University Press, 1995), 111–27, esp. 111. J. K. Elliott, "Mark 1.1–3: A Later Addition to the Gospel?" *NTS* 46 (2000) 584–88, argued that these first verses were added to Mark later, perhaps due to the loss of the opening sheet (and the last sheet, if a single quire codex were involved). N. Clayton Croy, "Where the Gospel Text Begins: A Non-Theological Interpretation of Mark 1:1," *NovT* 43 (2001) 105–27, proposed that Mark's present first verse was added—to replace some lost and unknown material—to show scribes where this (defective) Gospel began.

17. See Collins, "Establishing the Text," for the entire discussion, and the summary on p. 125.

18. Parker, *Living Text of the Gospels,* 75–94.

19. Ibid., 75.
20. Ibid., 209; on accuracy in transmission, see further 199–200.
21. Ibid., 76.
22. Ibid., 76–77.
23. Ibid., 78–79.
24. Ibid., 84–85.
25. Ibid., 84.
26. Ibid., 90–91.
27. Ibid., 89.
28. Ibid., 91, 92, 93; cf. 183.
29. Ibid., 94.
30. Ibid., 209; cf. 208.
31. Ibid., 212; for "single" see 76, 91, esp. 92, 94, 183, 208.
32. E.g., Michael W. Holmes, "Reasoned Eclecticism in New Testament Textual Criticism," in *The Text of the New Testament in Contemporary Research: Essays on the Status Quaestionis*, ed. B. D. Ehrman and M. W. Holmes (SD 46; Grand Rapids: Eerdmans, 1995), 343; Epp, "Issues in New Testament Textual Criticism," 20–34.
33. In addition to Parker, *Living Text of the Gospels*, and the discussion above, see Ehrman, *Orthodox Corruption of Scripture*, in general, and his "The Text as Window: New Testament Manuscripts and the Social History of Early Christianity," in *The Text of the New Testament in Contemporary Research*, ed. Ehrman and Holmes, 361–79; cf. Epp, "Multivalence of the Term 'Original Text,'" 258–60, 264–66.
34. Epp, "Issues in New Testament Textual Criticism," 60.
35. See ibid., 25–34, for a summary of the current status of these issues.

2. Variant Readings in Passages concerning Gender Issues
1. Bart D. Ehrman, *The Orthodox Corruption of Scripture: The Effect of Early Christological Controversies on the Text of the New Testament* (New York: Oxford University Press, 1993), passim.
2. E.g., Eldon Jay Epp, *The Theological Tendency of Codex Bezae Cantabrigiensis in Acts* (SNTSMS 3; Cambridge: Cambridge University Press, 1966).
3. See Joël Delobel, "Textual Criticism and Exegesis: Siamese Twins?" in *New Testament Textual Criticism, Exegesis, and Early Church History: A Discussion of Methods*, ed. Barbara Aland and Joël Delobel (Kampen: Kok Pharos, 1994), for a summary.
4. David C. Parker, *The Living Text of the Gospels* (Cambridge: Cambridge University Press, 1997), 93, 183, respectively.
5. Ibid., 92–94; 172–74; esp. 208–12.

6. Delobel, "Textual Criticism and Exegesis: Siamese Twins?" 110 n. 40. His discussion of 1 Cor 14:34–35 is on 110–11.

Another defense of the Pauline character of 1 Cor 14:34-35 suggests that Paul had a restricted, special circumstance in view—in the interest of church order some women should be silent sometimes, that is, when learning in public they must not be loud and disruptive: Craig S. Keener, *Paul, Women & Wives: Marriage and Women's Ministry in the Letters of Paul* (Peabody, Mass.: Hendrickson, 1992) 70–100, esp. 79–88. Another argues that the passage was excised from 1 Corinthians by Marcion or a Marcionite: David W. Bryce, "'As in All the Churches of the Saints: A Text-Critical Study of 1 Corinthians 14:34-35," *Lutheran Theological Journal* [Australia] 31 (1997) 31–39, esp. 36–38. This was a response to Peter F. Lockwood, "Does 1 Corinthians 14:34–35 Exclude Women from the Pastoral Office?" *Lutheran Theological Journal* [Australia] 30 (1996) 30–38, who had answered his own question in the negative.

7. Hans Conzelmann, *1 Corinthians: A Commentary on the First Epistle to the Corinthians* (Hermeneia; Philadelphia: Fortress Press, 1975), 246. Conzelmann was much alone in defining the interpolated segment as vv. 33b–36; most treat it as vv. 34–35, e.g., Jerome Murphy-O'Connor, "Interpolations in 1 Corinthians," *CBQ* 48 (1986) 90; Gordon D. Fee, *The First Epistle to the Corinthians* (NICNT; Grand Rapids: Eerdmans, 1987), 699 n. 4.

8. Gordon D. Fee, *First Epistle to the Corinthians*, 699–708; idem, *God's Empowering Presence: The Holy Spirit in the Letters of Paul* (Peabody, Mass.: Hendrickson, 1994), 272–81. D. A. Carson, "'Silent in the Churches': On the Role of Women in 1 Corinthians 14:33b–36," in *Recovering Biblical Manhood and Womanhood: A Response to Evangelical Feminism*, ed. J. Piper and W. Grudem (Wheaton, Ill.: Crossway, 1991), 141–45, argued authenticity against Fee; Curt Niccum, "The Voice of the Manuscripts on the Silence of Women: The External Evidence for 1 Cor 14.34–5," *NTS* 43 (1997) 242–55, also attempted to counter Fee's view (and Payne's; see below).

9. E.g., Gottfried Fitzer, *Das Weib schweige in der Gemeinde: Über den unpaulinischen Charakter der mulier-taceat Verse in 1. Korinther 14* (Theologische Existenz Heute 10; Munich: Kaiser, 1963); Wm. O. Walker, "1 Corinthians 11:2–16 and Paul's Views regarding Women," *JBL* 94 (1975) 95 (n. 6 provided the basic arguments and bibliography of eight scholars supporting interpolation); Murphy-O'Connor, "Interpolations in 1 Corinthians," 90–92; Jacobus H. Petzer, "Reconsidering the Silent Women of Corinth: A Note on 1 Corinthians 14:34–35,

Theologia evangelica 26 (1993) 132–38; Jouette M. Bassler, "1 Corinthians," in *Women's Bible Commentary, Expanded Edition,* ed. Carol A. Newsom and Sharon H. Ringe (Louisville: Westminster John Knox, 1998), 418–19, who asks how the women in Romans 16 can function as "co-workers" (Prisca, Mary, Junia, Tryphaena, and Tryphosa) or as a "deacon" (Phoebe) if they cannot speak out in the assembly. See also Andrie du Toit, "Die swyggebod van 1 Korintiërs 14:34–35 weer eens onder die loep," *Hervormde Teologiese Studies* 57 (2001) 172–86.

That vv. 34–35 were interpolated from another Pauline letter was the view of Robert W. Allison, "Let Women Be Silent in the Churches (1 Cor. 14.33b–36): What Did Paul Really Say, and What Did It Mean?" *JSNT* 32 (1988) 27–60, esp. 44–48; Allison discussed an array of other views as well.

10. Other studies that utilize text criticism include E. Earle Ellis, "The Silenced Wives of Corinth (1 Cor. 14:34–5)," in *New Testament Textual Criticism, Its Significance for Exegesis: Essays in Honour of Bruce M. Metzger,* ed. E. J. Epp and G. D. Fee (Oxford: Clarendon Press, 1981), 213–20 (see the correction noted in P. B. Payne, *NTS* 41 [1995] 246); Antoinette Clark Wire, *The Corinthian Women Prophets: A Reconstruction through Paul's Rhetoric* (Minneapolis: Fortress Press, 1990), 149–58, 229–32; cf. her "1 Corinthians," in *Searching the Scriptures, Volume Two: A Feminist Commentary,* ed. Elisabeth Schüssler Fiorenza (New York: Crossroad, 1994), 186–87; J. M. Ross, "Floating Words: Their Significance for Textual Criticism," *NTS* 38 (1992) 155–56; see Bruce M. Metzger (for the Editorial Committee), *A Textual Commentary on the Greek New Testament* (2d ed.; Stuttgart: Deutsche Bibelgesellschaft/United Bible Societies, 1994), 499–500. Cf. Neal M. Flanagan and Edwina Hunter Snyder, "Did Paul Put Down Women in 1 Cor 14: 34–36?" *BTB* 11 (1981) 10–12, who viewed vv. 34–35 as Paul's quotation of the words of "the men" in v. 36 whom he is chiding. Daniel C. Arichea, "The Silence of Women in the Church: Theology and Translation in 1 Corinthians 14.33b–36," *BT* (Technical Papers) 46 (1995) 101–12, leaned in this direction also.

11. Delobel, *Textual Criticism and Exegesis,* 110–11.

12. On manuscript 88, see Antoinette Clark Wire, *The Corinthian Women Prophets,* 151; Philip B. Payne, "Ms. 88 as Evidence for a Text without 1 Cor 14.34–5," *NTS* 44 (1998) 154.

13. Philip B. Payne, "Fuldensis, Sigla for Variants in Vaticanus, and 1 Cor 14.34–5," *NTS* 41 (1995) 250–51. Payne reported (p. 251 and n. 40) that the separate paragraph for vv. 34–35 was marked "in every other ancient Greek ms. of this passage I have been able to find."

14. Ibid., 241–50. Curt Niccum, "Voice of the Manuscripts," 246–47, attempted an alternative position.

15. Payne, "Fuldensis, Sigla for Variants in Vaticanus," 250–60 + 1 plate.

16. Philip B. Payne and Paul Canart, "The Originality of Text-Critical Symbols in Codex Vaticanus," *NovT* 42 (2000) 106–7, 113. See also idem, "'Umlauts' Matching the Original Ink of Codex Vaticanus: Do They Mark the Location of Textual Variants?" in *Le manuscrit B de la Bible (Vaticanus gr. 1209): Introduction au facsimilé, Actes du Colloque de Genève (11 juin 2001), Contributions supplémentaires*, ed. Patrick Andrist (Lausanne: Èditions du Zèbre, 2004) 191–214.

17. Payne, "Fuldensis, Sigla for Variants in Vaticanus," 251–60.

18. Ibid., 252, 257; Payne and Canart, "Originality of Text-Critical Symbols," 110, 112–13.

19. Niccum, "Voice of the Manuscripts," 244–46. His critique of Payne was effectively countered in Payne and Canart, "The Originality of Text-Critical Symbols," passim, but especially 109 n. 25.

20. Payne and Canart, "Originality of Text-Critical Symbols," 107–9.

21. Ibid., 109–10; 112–13. Payne, "Fuldensis, Sigla for Variants in Vaticanus," 257, provided instructive parallels between John 7:53—8:11 and 1 Cor 14:34–35 that strengthen the arguments that both were interpolations. Marlene Crüsemann, "Irredeemably Hostile to Women: Anti-Jewish Elements in the Exegesis of the Dispute about Women's Right to Speak (1 Cor. 14.34–35)," *JSNT* 79 (2000) 19–36, provides valuable current and history-of-exegesis insights on the subject, though it is not obvious how her claim that "it is especially in proponents of the interpolation hypothesis that a structural anti-Judaism comes to light" (33) can be charged against the text-critical argument for interpolation that is offered in our essay.

22. J. Edward Miller, "Some Observations on the Text-Critical Function of the Umlauts in Vaticanus, with Special Attention to 1 Corinthians 14.34–35," *JSNT* 26 (2003) 217–36.

23. Philip B. Payne, "The Text-Critical Function of the Umlauts in Vaticanus, with Special Attention to 1 Corinthians 14.34–35: A Response to J. Edward Miller," *JSNT* 27 (2004) 105–12.

24. Payne, "Ms. 88 as Evidence for a Text without 1 Cor 14.34–5," 152–58.

25. See a summary of the problems in Fee, *First Epistle to the Corinthians*, 701–5. D. W. Odell-Scott presents a plausible alternate view for the dislocation, which affirms that Paul indeed wrote vv. 34–35 in the traditional position but that they were removed and interpolated

after v. 40; the twist, however, according to Odell-Scott, is that vv. 34–35 were being quoted by Paul from a factional Corinthian group and were refuted by Paul in v. 36: Paul was rejecting the silencing of women. Subsequently, "editors," such as those of manuscripts D, G, and 88, intent on reflecting church views of women in their day, moved vv. 34–35 to elaborate the "decency and order" principle enunciated in v. 40. See his "Editorial Dilemma: The Interpolation of 1 Cor 14:34–35 in the Western Manuscripts of D, G, and 88," *BTB* 30 (2000) 68–74, and his earlier articles cited there: *BTB* 13 (1983) 90–3; 17 (1987) 100–3. Michel Gourgues, "Who Is Misogynist: Paul or Certain Corinthians? Note on 1 Corinthians 14:33b–36," in *Women Also Journeyed with Him: Feminist Perspectives on the Bible*, ed. Gérald Caron et al. (Collegeville, Minn.: Liturgical Press, 2000), 117–24, argues for the same "Corinthian slogan" view, though Gourgues does not treat the text-critical aspects. Another recent view is from Graham Clarke, "As in All the Churches of the Saints," *BT* 52 (2001) 144–47.

Part II: Junia/Junias in Romans 16:7

1. See Peter Lampe, *From Paul to Valentinus: Christians at Rome in the First Two Centuries*, trans. Michael Steinhauser, ed. Marshall D. Johnson (Minneapolis: Fortress Press, 2003) 166–67; cf. 187–95.

2. My purpose is not to join the conversation about who was the first woman apostle but to explore the case for Junia as the first woman *to be called* an apostle in the New Testament literature that became canonical. Currently in scholarship, as well as in popular media, Mary Magdalene has emerged as an apostle—more specifically as both "the first woman apostle," and "the first apostle"; note the titles of two fine contributions to scholarship in 2003: Karen L. King, *The Gospel of Mary of Magdala: Jesus and the First Woman Apostle* (Santa Rosa, Calif.: Polebridge, 2003), esp. 141–54; 175–90; and Ann Graham Brock, *Mary Magdalene, the First Apostle: The Struggle for Authority* (HTS 51; Cambridge, Mass.: Harvard University Press, 2003), esp. 1–18; 145–48; 161–75.

3. The Lexical Form and Introductory Matters

1. A. T. Robertson, *A Grammar of the Greek New Testament in the Light of Historical Research* (Nashville: Broadman, 1934), 172. Only here and in M.-J. Lagrange, *Saint Paul: Épître aux Romains* (Ebib; Paris: Gabalda, 1914, 1931⁴; reprint, 1950), 366, have I seen the explicit proposal that Junias is an abbreviation of a *Greek* name. Lagrange accents differently: Ἰουνιᾶνος.

2. Peter Lampe, "Junias," in *ABD* 3:1127; cf. idem, "Iunia/Iunias: Sklavenherkunft im Kreise der vorpaulinischen Apostel (Röm 16 7),"

ZNW 76 (1985) 132–34. Lampe's count of occurrences, including inscriptions, was more than 250; idem, "The Roman Christians of Romans 16," in Karl P. Donfried, ed., *The Romans Debate* (rev. and exp. ed.; Peabody, Mass.: Hendrickson, 1991), 226; of all the names in Rom 16:3–16, only three were found more often than Junia: Julia (1400+), Hermes (640), and Rufus (ca. 374). Metzger, *Textual Commentary*[2], 475, reported similarly that "the female Latin name Junia occurs more than 250 times in Greek and Latin inscriptions found in Rome alone." Richard S. Cervin, "A Note regarding the Name 'Junia(s)' in Romans 16.7," *NTS* 40 (1994) 468 and notes, provided primary sources for the name Junia, as did Lampe. Very recently, Linda Belleville, "'Ιουνιαν ... ἐπίσημοι ἐν τοῖς ἀποστόλοις: A Re-examination of Romans 16.7 in Light of Primary Source Materials," *NTS* 51 (2005) 234; 240–41, searched both *TLG*, a literary database, and *PHI*, a non-literary database, and found six extrabiblical occurrences of Junia in the former and numerous examples in the latter, of which she gives some twenty-one examples from Rome and other localities, with many from the first century C.E.

3. Peter Lampe, "Junias," in *ABD* 3:1127. See further below; the proposed (but unlikely) exceptions also will be discussed later.

4. John Thorley, "Junia, a Woman Apostle," *NovT* 38 (1996) 20; note that to his carefully worded statement must be added: "However, the ending -A (with or without an additional accusative sign) can, in all of the languages of the early translations, also be used for some masculine names" (ibid.). This subject is discussed further below.

5. BAGD, ad loc.; BDF, §125 (2). Though the current editions are quoted here, the older editions and their predecessors contained virtually the same language, in the case of BDF, back to Friedrich Blass, *Grammatik des neutestamentlichen Griechisch* (Göttingen, 1896); rev. Albert Debrunner (1913[4]–1954[9]); rev. Friedrich Rehkopf (1976[14]); also the English trans. of Blass by Henry St. John Thackeray, *Grammar of New Testament Greek* (London: Macmillan, 1898), 71 n. 4; and in the case of BAGD, back to Erwin Preuschen, *Vollständiges griechisch-deutsches Handwörterbuch* (Giessen: Töpelmann, 1910). See the discussion below and the next note.

6. Only 'Ιουνίας appeared in K. L. W. Grimm, *Lexicon Graeco-Latinum in libros Novi Testamenti* (Leipzig: Arnold, 1862, 1879[2]); Preuschen, *Handwörterbuch*; and Blass, *Grammatik*. However, Joseph Henry Thayer, *Greek-English Lexicon of the New Testament, Being Grimm's Wilke's Clavis Novi Testamenti* (New York: Harper, 1886, corr. ed., 1889), listed 'Ιουνιᾶς as an alternate to 'Ιουνίας, -α, ὁ; whereas the sixth (and latest) German edition of Bauer, Kurt Aland and Bar-

bara Aland, eds., *Griechisch-deutsches Wörterbuch* (Berlin: de Gruyter, 1988), 770, listed Ἰουνίας (masculine) as an alternative to Ἰουνιᾶς. Curiously, Alford, as in other ways, was an early exception, for (in his vol. 2, 1852) he read Ἰουνιᾶν in his text and, in a note, gave Ἰουνίαν as the feminine alternative: Henry Alford, *The Greek New Testament, with a Critically Revised Text; . . . and a Critical and Exegetical Commentary* (4 vols.; London: Rivingtons; Cambridge: Deighton, Bell, 1844–57), 2.467 (= 1877[7]).

7. See BDF §125 (1).

8. Peter Lampe, *From Paul to Valentinus: Christians at Rome in the First Two Centuries*, trans. Michael Steinhauser, ed. Marshall D. Johnson (Minneapolis: Fortress Press, 2003), 169, 178.

9. William Sanday and Arthur C. Headlam, *A Critical and Exegetical Commentary on the Epistle to the Romans* (ICC; Edinburgh: T. & T. Clark, 1895; 1902[5]), 422–23; C. E. B. Cranfield, *The Epistle to the Romans* (ICC; 2 vols.; Edinburgh: T. & T. Clark, 1979; reprint, 1994), 2.788; the data are found in BDF, §125 and §125 (1), and A. T. Robertson, *Grammar*, 172–73. See now Lampe, *From Paul to Valentinus*, 164–83; on the "-anus" ending, 176–77.

10. Joseph Barber Lightfoot, *On a Fresh Revision of the English New Testament* (London: Macmillan, 1871[1], 1891[3]), 179. James Denney, *St. Paul's Epistle to the Romans*, in *The Expositor's Greek Testament*, ed. W. R. Nicoll (5 vols.; London: Hodder and Stoughton, 1897–1910; reprint, Grand Rapids: Eerdmans, 1956), 2.719, asserted that "Ἰουνίαν may be masculine (from Ἰουνίας, or Ἰουνιᾶς contraction of Junianus), or feminine (from Ἰουνία): probably the former."

11. Sanday and Headlam, *Romans*, 422. Cranfield, *Romans*, 2.788, took Sanday and Headlam to task for asserting that, while Junia was a common name, "Junias . . . is less usual as a man's name"—when in fact the name Junias has not been found.

12. Lagrange, *Épître aux Romains*, 366.

13. W. F. Moulton and A. S. Geden, *A Concordance to the Greek Testament* (Edinburgh: T. & T. Clark, [1]1897, [3]1926), ad loc.

14. K. Aland, *Vollständige Konkordanz zum griechischen Neuen Testament* (ANTF 4; 2 vols.; Berlin/New York: de Gruyter, 1975–83), ad loc.

15. Robert D. Sider, ed., *Collected Works of Erasmus, Vol. 56: New Testament Scholarship, Annotations on Romans* (Toronto: University of Toronto Press, 1994), 427.

16. J. Wordsworth and H. J. White, *Novum Testamentum Domini nostri Jesu Christi Latine* (3 vols.; Oxford: Clarendon, 1898–1954; Epistles vol., 1913), 147.

17. Richard Francis Weymouth, *The Resultant Greek Testament* (London: James Clarke, 1886, 1905⁵).

18. Idem, *The New Testament in Modern Speech: An Idiomatic Translation into Every-day English from the Text of 'The Resultant Greek Testament'* (London: J. Clarke, 1903; 1929⁵).

19. F. J. A. Hort, *Prolegomena to St Paul's Epistles to the Romans and the Ephesians* (London: Macmillan, 1895), 9.

20. Benjamin Wilson, *The Emphatic Diaglott Containing the Original Greek Text of What Is Commonly Styled the New Testament . . . with an Interlineary Word for Word English Translation* (Geneva, Ill.: by the author, 1864); the book was reprinted in 1902, when it was adopted by the Watch Tower Bible and Tract Society and often reprinted by them. I refer to the 1942 ed., published in Brooklyn.

21. Weymouth, *Resultant Greek Testament*, 422.

22. Alford, *Greek New Testament*, 2:467 (1852¹, 1877⁷).

23. "Julia" is a textual variant for "Junia" in Rom 16:7, found notably in 𝔓46, and in several other witnesses, and it occurs also in Rom 16:15 (where, curiously but understandably, "Junia" is a variant in a few manuscripts). Julia is of interest, as noted below, only as confirmation that a female name stood in Rom 16:7.

A conjecture that Joanna (only in Luke 8:3 and 24:10) is to be identified with Junia of Rom 16:7 has been proposed and argued at length by Richard Bauckham, *Gospel Women: Studies of the Named Women in the Gospels* (Grand Rapids: Eerdmans, 2002), 165–86.

24. Lampe, *From Paul to Valentinus*, 169, 175.

4. Junia in Early Christian Writers—and Beyond

1. Joseph A. Fitzmyer, *Romans* (AB 33; New York: Doubleday, 1993), 737–38; see his references to original sources.

2. Linda Belleville, "Ἰουνιαν . . . ἐπίσημοι ἐν τοῖς ἀποστόλοις: A Re-examination of Romans 16.7 in Light of Primary Source Materials," *NTS* 51 (2005) 232 n. 1, which also provides references to original sources.

3. I use the translation of Bernadette Brooten, "'Junia . . . Outstanding among the Apostles' (Romans 16:7)," in *Women Priests: A Catholic Commentary on the Vatican Declaration*, ed. L. and A. Swidler (New York: Paulist, 1977), 141; cf. the German trans.: "'Junia . . . Hervorragend unter den Aposteln' (Röm 16,7)," in *Frauenbefreiung: Biblische und theologische Argumente*, ed. Elisabeth Moltmann-Wendel (Munich: Chr. Kaiser, 1978, 1982³), 148.

4. I have this (and the next) reference and translation from Belleville, "A Re-examination of Romans 16.7," 234–35.

5. Ibid., 235. She notes also that Oecumenius (early sixth century) and Theophylact (fl. 1070–1081) recognize "that a woman is not only named 'an apostle' . . . but also 'notable among them'" (236).

6. E.g., Charles Ernest Burland Cranfield, *The Epistle to the Romans* (2 vols.; ICC; Edinburgh: T. & T. Clark, 1979; reprint, 1994), 2:788; James D. G. Dunn, *Romans 9–16* (WBC 38; Dallas: Word, 1988), 894; cf. "The male name Junias is unattested anywhere," Metzger, *Textual Commentary*[2], 475. Also, Richard S. Cervin, "A Note regarding the Name 'Junia(s)' in Romans 16.7," *NTS* 40 (1994) 466–67; see 468–69 on "Junius," an ancient, common Latin name; not so with "Junias."

7. Caroline P. Hammond Bammel, *Der Römerbriefkommentar des Origenes: Kritische Ausgabe der Übersetzung Rufins* (Vetus Latina, Aus der Geschichte der lateinischen Bibel 16, 33, 34; 3 vols.; Freiburg: Herder, 1990, 1997, 1998), 836–37, 853. See her print-out, with a brief apparatus, of Rufinus's text of Romans, in her *Der Römerbrieftext des Rufin und seine Origenes-Übersetzung* (Vetus Latina, Aus der Geschichte der lateinischen Bibel 10; Freiburg: Herder, 1985), 536, which read *Iunia* at Rom 16:7, with no variants cited except the usual *Iulia*. For a pre-Hammond Bammel assessment of Rufinus's translation, see Valentin Fàbrega, "War Junia(s), der hervorragende Apostel (Rom. 16,7), eine Frau?" JAC 27/28 (1984/1985) 58–9.

8. *In ep. ad Romanos* (PL 111:1607–8); I rely on Fitzmyer, *Romans*, 737–38.

9. Fàbrega, "War Junia(s), der hervorragende Apostel (Rom. 16,7), eine Frau?" 59 n. 51; cf. Lampe, "Roman Christians of Romans 16," 223, who said that Fàbrega "erroneously relies on Migne's reading 'Junias' in Origen's commentary, although all other textual witnesses to this commentary . . . offer 'Junia.'"

10. John Piper and Wayne Grudem, "An Overview of Central Concerns," in *Recovering Biblical Manhood and Womanhood*, ed. Piper and Grudem (Wheaton, Ill.: Crossway, 1991), 79–80 and 479 n. 19. See the critique of Richard Bauckham, *Gospel Women: Studies of the Named Women in the Gospels* (Grand Rapids: Eerdmans, 2002), 166 n. 242; and Belleville, "A Re-examination of Romans 16.7," 235.

11. Cervin, "Note regarding the Name 'Junia(s)' in Romans 16.7," 466 n. 13. On the Latin Junia, see Lampe, *From Paul to Valentinus*, 169, 176–77; Belleville, "A Re-examination of Romans 16.7," 234.

12. Brooten, "Junia . . . Outstanding among the Apostles," 141–42. Peter Lampe, "Junia/Junias: Sklavenherkunft im Kreise der vorpaulinischen Apostel (Röm 16,7)," ZNW 76 (1985) 132 n. 1, claimed that G. Lohfink "clearly erred" when he called Aegidius the first to identify

Ἰουνιαν as a man, because the minuscules (e.g. 33) so accent it [i.e., Ἰουνιᾶν] already in the ninth century. Lampe, however, in his later "Junias" in *ABD* 3:1127, properly reversed his position on minuscule 33, reporting that it has Ἰουνίαν, which Lampe took as explicitly feminine. Fitzmyer, *Romans*, 738, quoted Lampe's earlier article and followed that errant view.

13. See Brooten, "Junia . . . Outstanding among the Apostles," 141.

14. Jacobus Faber Stapulensis [Jacques LeFèvre d'Étaples], *S. Pauli epistolae XIV ex Vulgata, adiecta intelligentia ex graeco, cum commentariis* (facsimile reprint of the Paris edition of 1512; Stuttgart: Frommann-Holzboog, 1978), 104b–5.

15. Robert D. Sider, ed., *Collected Works of Erasmus, Vol. 42: New Testament Scholarship, Paraphrases on Romans and Galatians* (Toronto: University of Toronto Press, 1984), 88.

16. John Thorley, "Junia, A Woman Apostle," *NovT* 38 (1996) 21.

17. Ibid.

18. Ibid., 22.

19. Bonafatius Fischer, OSB, ed., *Novae Concordantiae Bibliorum Sacrorum iuxta vulgatam versionem critice editam* (5 vols.; Stuttgart: Frommann-Holzboog, 1977), 2777.

20. Martin Luther, *Church and Ministry*, Luther's Works 41, ed. Eric W. Gritsch (St. Louis: Concordia and Philadelphia: Fortress Press, 1966), 348.

21. Martin Luther, *Lectures on Romans*, Luther's Works 25, ed. Hilton C. Oswald (St. Louis: Concordia and Philadelphia: Fortress Press, 1972), 129.

22. S. L. Greenslade, ed., *The Cambridge History of the Bible*, Volume 3: *The West from the Reformation to the Present Day* (Cambridge: Cambridge University Press, 1963), 103.

23. Luise Schottroff, *Let the Oppressed Go Free: Feminine Perspectives on the New Testament* (Louisville: Westminster John Knox, 1993), 36. Belleville, "A Re-examination of Romans 16.7," 237 n. 24, reminds us that Luther used Erasmus's second edition of the Greek New Testament for his German translation, which reads Junia, "so the source of the masculine Junias may well reflect Luther's personal disposition against an apostolic attribution." On Luther's use of Erasmus, see Greenslade, *The West from the Reformation to the Present Day*, 3:99.

24. John Locke, *A Paraphrase and Notes on the Epistles of St Paul to the Galatians, 1 and 2 Corinthians, Romans, Ephesians*, ed. Arthur W. Wainwright (2 vols.; Oxford: Clarendon, 1987).

25. Ibid., 1:11–17.

26. Ibid., 2:601–3. There were no comments on these passages in his "Manuscript Notes," 733, "Textual Notes," 761, or "Explanatory Notes," 801–2.

27. Brooten, "Junia . . . Outstanding among the Apostles," 142. Her reference was to Drusius in *Critici Sacri* VII (Amsterdam, 1698) 930.

28. Brooten, "Junia . . . Outstanding among the Apostles," 142; she reported that the dissertation was specifically on "Andronicum et Juniam."

29. Peter Arzt, "Iunia oder Iunias? Zum textkritischen Hintergrund von Röm 16,7," in *Liebe zum Wort: Beiträge zur klassischen und biblischen Philologie, P. Ludger Bernhard OSB zum 80. Geburtstag dargebracht von Kollegen und Schülern,* ed. F. V. Reiterer and P. Eder (Salzburg: Otto Müller, 1993), 84 and n. 7. For Bentley, see Arthur Ayres Ellis, *Bentleii Critica Sacra* (Cambridge: Deighton, Bell, 1862) 31.

30. Other English versions that earlier used the word "men" include James Moffatt's *The New Testament: A New Translation* (1913): "they are men of note among the apostles"; Edgar J. Goodspeed's *The New Testament: An American Translation* (1923): "they are noted men among the missionaries"; later, J. B. Phillips, in his *Letters to Young Churches* (1947): "They are outstanding men among the messengers." These examples were collected by Roger L. Omanson, "Who's Who in Romans 16? Identifying Men and Women among the People Paul Sent Greetings To," *BT* 49 (1998) 432, though he does not mention the RSV (1946) or the *Amplified New Testament* (1958). Omanson reminds us also of Clarence Jordan's colorful *Cotton Patch Version of Paul's Epistles* (New York: Association Press, 1968): "Warm regards to Andy and Junior, my kinfolk and fellow captives, who are highly respected in ministerial circles." Omanson, 433, points out that the discussion on Andronicus and Junia(s) is "woefully inadequate" in Barclay M. Newman and Eugene A. Nida, *A Translator's Handbook on Paul's Letter to the Romans* (Helps for Translators, 14; London and Stuttgart: United Bible Societies, 1973), ad loc.

5. The Contracted-Name Theory

1. Bruce M. Metzger (for the Editorial Committee), *A Textual Commentary on the Greek New Testament* (2d ed.; Stuttgart: Deutsche Bibelgesellschaft and United Bible Societies, 1994), 475.

2. Quoting here BAGD, ad loc.; Metzger's *Textual Commentary*[2] refers to the sixth (and latest) German edition of Bauer's *Wörterbuch,* ed. Kurt and Barbara Aland, 770–71, which reads exactly as BAGD.

3. BDF §125 (2). The other reference was to Archibald T. Robertson, *A Grammar of the Greek New Testament in the Light of Historical Research* (Nashville: Broadman, 1934), who said that the name is "sometimes taken as feminine Ἰουνία, Rom. 16:7," but "may be Ἰουνιᾶς as abbreviation of Ἰουνιανός," that is, from the Greek rather than the Latin (p. 172).

4. Erwin Preuschen, *Vollständiges griechisch-deutsches Handwörterbuch* (Giessen: Töpelmann, 1910).

5. Friedrich Blass, *Grammatik des neutestamentlichen Griechisch* (Göttingen, 1896; rev. by Albert Debrunner, 1913⁴–1954⁹; rev. by Friedrich Rehkopf, 1976¹⁴); English trans. by Henry St. John Thackeray, *Grammar of New Testament Greek* (London: Macmillan, 1898), 71 n. 4 = §29.

6. K. L. W. Grimm, *Lexicon Graeco-Latinum in libros Novi Testamenti* (Leipzig: Arnold, 1862, 1879²).

7. Joseph H. Thayer, *Greek-English Lexicon of the New Testament, Being Grimm's Wilke's Clavis Novi Testamenti* (New York: Harper, 1886; cor. ed., 1889), ad loc.

8. Commentaries that referred to the contracted-name theory in an approving manner or as a possibility include those by Henry Alford, *The Greek New Testament, with a Critically Revised Text; . . . and a Critical and Exegetical Commentary* (4 vols.; London: Rivingtons; Cambridge: Deighton, Bell, 1844–1857; 1877⁷), 2:467; William Sanday and A. C. Hedlam, *A Critical and Exegetical Commentary on the Epistle to the Romans* (ICC; Edinburgh: T. & T. Clark, 1895; 1902⁵), 422–23; M.-J. Lagrange, *Saint Paul: Épître aux Romains* (Ebib; Paris: Gabalda, 1916¹, 1931⁴; repr. 1950), 366: "possibly" (but Junia is feminine); Otto Michel, *Der Brief an die Römer* (KEK; Göttingen: Vandenhoeck & Ruprecht, 1955¹; 1978⁵), 475: (accepted); C. E. B. Cranfield, *The Epistle to the Romans* (2 vols.; ICC; Edinburgh: T & T Clark, 1979; reprint, 1994), 788: "perhaps" (but, for Cranfield, Junia is feminine); Joseph A. Fitzmyer, *Romans* (AB 33; New York: Doubleday, 1993), 738: possible (but Junia is feminine). James D. G. Dunn, *Romans 9–16* (WBC 38; Dallas: Word, 1988), 894, rejects the view.

9. Richard S. Cervin, "A Note regarding the Name 'Junia(s)' in Romans 16.7," *NTS* 40 (1994) 464–70; John Thorley, "Junia, A Woman Apostle," *NovT* 38 (1996) 18–29. Thorley did not appear to know of Cervin's article. The importance of the point is illustrated, e.g., in Thomas R. Schreiner, "The Valuable Ministries of Women in the Context of Male Leadership," in *Recovering Biblical Manhood and Womanhood*, ed. Piper and Grudem 221, who appealed to the list of contracted names *in Greek* provided by Robertson, *Grammar*, 171–73 (which, on

p. 172, included Ἰουνιᾶς as the abbreviation of Ἰουνιανός). Cf. p. 80 in Piper and Grudem.

10. Cervin, "Note regarding the Name 'Junia(s),'" 466.

11. Ibid., 468–69. His numerous examples have been left out of this quotation. Now see also Peter Lampe, *From Paul to Valentinus: Christians at Rome in the First Two Centuries*, trans. Michael Steinhauser, ed. Marshall D. Johnson (Minneapolis: Fortress Press, 2003), 165 n. 39; 176–77.

12. Lampe, ibid., points out that *Junianus* occurs twenty-one times in Rome, that *Junias* "could be a short form" (169), but that there are no examples of *Junias* as a short form of *Junianus*, and, finally, that Junia is feminine is "most probable" (176).

13. See chap. 3, n. 10, above.

14. Thorley, "Junia, a Woman Apostle," 24. On the alleged occurrence of Junias in Epiphanius, see the discussion above.

15. Ibid. Thorley's critique of Ray R. Schulz, "Romans 16:7: Junia or Junias?" *ExpT* 98 (1986/87) 108–10, is worth noting, especially since it is one of three references provided in the UBS *Textual Commentary*². (1) Schulz asserted that the Greek -ᾶς form in the first declension is "extremely rare" (109); Thorley was emphatic that this is "quite wrong"—it is common (24 and n. 13). (2) Schulz said "Latin names of endearment normally lengthen" (109), as Prisca and its diminutive, Priscilla; Thorley responded: "This is true of pure Latin names, but here we have a Latin name with a suggested *Greek* ending which *shortened* the name" (24 n. 14). Bernadette J. Brooten, "'Junia . . . Outstanding among the Apostles' (Romans 16:7)," in *Women Priests: A Catholic Commentary on the Vatican Declaration*, ed. Leonard S. and Arlene Swidler (New York: Paulist, 1977), 142–43, earlier made a claim similar to Schulz's in refuting the hypocoristic theory. (3) Schulz claimed that Junias could be a contraction of a female name (110); Thorley said "this is certainly not so" (24 n. 14).

16. I.e., the name that is to be shortened.

17. Thorley, "Junia, a Woman Apostle," 24–25. See his examples, further evidence and references, and treatment of the two apparent exceptions.

18. Ibid., 25. P.Oxy. III.502 is a contract, dated 164 C.E., for the lease of a house at Oxyrhynchus, for which "Iulas son of Didymus" acted as intermediary.

19. Ibid., 23; cf. 19–23. The note of caution was due to the fact that, while all of these early translations "without exception transcribe the name in what can be taken as a feminine form," none gives a positive sign for a masculine name, even though the ending -A also can be used

in all of these languages "for some masculine names" (p. 20). Unknown to Thorley, in 1993 Peter Arzt, "Iunia oder Iunias? Zum textkritischen Hintergrund von Röm 16,7," in *Liebe zum Wort: Beiträge zur klassischen und biblischen Philologie,* ed. F. V. Reiterer and P. Eder (Salzburg: Otto Müller, 1993), 94–95, found that the Syriac and Coptic versions and all Old Latin and Vulgate manuscripts refer to a woman, except R₃ (Codex Reginensis, eighth century), which has *Iulius.*

20. Peter Lampe, "The Roman Christians of Romans 16," in *The Romans Debate,* ed. Karl P. Donfried (Peabody, Mass.: Hendrickson, 1991)," 223; idem, *From Paul to Valentinus,* 165 n. 39.

21. Brooten, "Junia . . . Outstanding among the Apostles," 142.

6. Junia/Junias in Current Greek New Testaments

1. As John Thorley, "Junia, A Woman Apostle," *NovT* 38 (1996), 24 n. 12, pointed out, the accent can be seen in the famous minuscule 33 (ninth century) in Kurt Aland and Barbara Aland, eds., *The Text of the New Testament* (2d ed.; Grand Rapids: Eerdmans; Leiden: Brill, 1989), first line of plate 36, p. 143. Unknown to Thorley, Peter Arzt, "Iunia oder Iunias? Zum textkritischen Hintergrund von Röm 16,7," in *Liebe zum Wort: Beiträge zur klassischen und biblischen Philologie,* ed. F. V. Reiterer and P. Eder (Salzburg: Otto Müller, 1993), 89–94, in 1993 examined the nearly seventy "most important minuscules" (those in the Alands' categories I, II, and III) at the Münster Institut für Neutestamentliche Textforschung and found that *every one* reads Ἰουνίαν (except three that read Ἰουλίαν).

2. UBS⁴, p. 3*.

3. Bruce M. Metzger (for the Editorial Committee), *A Textual Commentary on the Greek New Testament* (1st ed.; London: United Bible Societies, 1972), 539.

4. Metzger, *Textual Commentary*², 476.

5. For cop^sa, see U.-K. Plisch, "Die Apostelin Junia: Das exegetische Problem in Röm 16.7 im Licht von Nestle-Aland²⁷ und der sahidischen Überlieferung," *NTS* 42 (1996) 477–78. For the minuscules, which date from the ninth to the seventeenth centuries, see Arzt, "Iunia oder Iunias?" 89–94. Reuben J. Swanson, in *New Testament Manuscripts: Variant Readings Arranged in Horizontal Lines against Codex Vaticanus: Romans* (Wheaton, Ill.: Tyndale House, 2001), 256, 286, reported that the tenth-century minuscule 1837 reads Ἰουνῖαν, which clearly is not Ἰουνιᾶν (masculine), but most likely represents Ἰουνίαν.

6. To which should be added minuscules 606 1718 2685, as reported in K. Aland, ed., *Text und Textwert der griechischen Handschriften des*

Neuen Testaments, II: Die paulinischen Briefe, Band 1: Allgemeines, Römerbrief und Ergänzungsliste (Berlin: de Gruyter, 1991), 434, and minuscule 6 apud Arzt, "Iunia oder Iunias?" 91.

7. My conclusion that this list is given for information only and not as textual support is based on the fact that, in the N-A[27] (1993) apparatus, the list of majuscules introduced by *sine acc.* is separated by a broken vertical line (see N-A[27], p. 53*) and thereby distinguished from the preceding evidence supporting the feminine form.

8. A minor point, perhaps, but there is no broken vertical line (see the preceding note) in the apparatus between the list of unaccented manuscripts and the preceding evidence supporting the feminine reading (which consists of B[2] D[2] 𝔭[vid] L 33 1739 1881 M).

9. E.g., no † has been placed in the apparatus to indicate a change from the text of the twenty-fifth edition (see N-A[27], p. 57*); nor is there any such indication in UBS[4(1998)]; and no list of changes appears in the *Bericht der Hermann Kunst-Stiftung zur Förderung der neutestamentlichen Textforschung für die Jahre 1995 bis 1998*, ed. Hermann Kunst (Munich: Hermann Kunst-Stiftung 1998), though, e.g., it updates the standard list of New Testament manuscripts.

7. Junia/Junias in Past Editions of Nestle, Nestle-Aland, and UBS

1. On the importance of the thirteenth edition, see Kurt Aland and Barbara Aland, *The Text of the New Testament: An Introduction to the Critical Editions and to the Theory and Practice of Modern Textual Criticism* (2d ed.; Grand Rapids: Eerdmans; Leiden: Brill, 1989), 20–22.

2. I have not checked the editions of Erwin Nestle for 1930[14] or 1932[15].

3. I cannot account for all the discrepancies between this list and the witnesses cited for the feminine in UBS[4], especially for the versional witnesses in UBS[1,2,3], none of which appears in UBS[4]. The assumption is that the Committee completely reworked this entry, as implied in the discussion in Bruce M. Metzger, *A Textual Commentary on the Greek New Testament* (2d ed.; Stuttgart: Deutsche Bibelgesellschaft and United Bible Societies, 1994), quoted below.

4. Kurt Aland, ed., *Text und Textwert der griechischen Handschriften des Neuen Testaments II: Die paulinischen Briefe, Band 1: Allgemeines, Römerbrief und Ergänzungsliste* (Berlin: de Gruyter, 1991), 433–35.

5. Peter Lampe, "Iunia/Iunias: Sklavenherkunft im Kreise der vorpaulinischen Apostel (Röm 16,7)," *ZNW* 76 (1985) 132.

6. Joseph A. Fitzmyer, *Romans*, AB 33 (New York: Doubleday, 1993), 738.

7. Peter Lampe, "Roman Christians of Romans 16," in *The Romans Debate*, ed. Karl P. Donfried (Peabody, Mass.: Hendrickson, 1991), 223; cf. now Peter Lampe, *From Paul to Valentinus: Christians at Rome in the First Two Centuries*, trans. Michael Steinhauser, ed. Marshall D. Johnson (Minneapolis: Fortress Press, 2003), 165 n. 39.

8. P. Lampe, "Junias," *ABD* 3:1127.

9. C. E. B. Cranfield, *The Epistle to the Romans* (2 vols.; ICC; Edinburgh: T. & T. Clark, 1979; reprint, 1994), 2:788. He acknowledged (p. vii) that he had used N-A[25] but then noted in the reprint any differences that N-A[26] presented. If he consulted also UBS[3] (1975), apparently the vast array of witnesses for the masculine did not impress him.

10. I was able to check the Eberhard Nestle editions of 1898[1], 1899[2], 1901[3], and 1906[6], but not 1903[4], 1904[5], or 1908[7] through 1912[9]; I checked Erwin Nestle 1920[11], 1927[13], 1936[16], 1941[17], and 1952[21], but not 1914[10], 1923[12], 1930[14], 1932[15], 1948[18], 1949[19], or 1950[20]; finally, I checked Nestle-Aland 1957[23], 1960[24], 1963[25], 1979[26], and 1993/1998[27], but not 1956[22].

8. The Accentuation of 'Ιουνιαν in Reference Works—and the Attendant Cultural Bias

1. Barclay M. Newman Jr., *A Concise Greek-English Dictionary of the New Testament* (Stuttgart: Deutsche Bibelgesellschaft/United Bible Societies, 1971), ad loc.; note that, curiously though understandably, the entry 'Ιουνιᾶς remains in the *Dictionary* bound with the UBS[4(1998)] even though no such accented form is any longer to be found in the *Greek New Testament* text or apparatus! Another curiosity is the entry "JUNIAS" (masculine) in the *ABD* (1992), yet the entry itself, by Peter Lampe (3.1127), treated almost exclusively and supported entirely Junia, the feminine form, except to report that the name Junias "did not exist in antiquity" and was unlikely to be a Greek abbreviation of the Latin name "Junianus."

2. Johannes P. Louw and Eugene A. Nida, eds., *Greek-English Lexicon of the New Testament Based on Semantic Domains* (2d ed.; 2 vols.; New York: United Bible Societies, 1989), 2:825 = §§ 93.177–78.

3. F. Wilbur Gingrich and Frederick W. Danker, *Shorter Lexicon of the Greek New Testament* (2d ed.; Chicago: University of Chicago Press, 1983).

4. Bruce M. Metzger, *A Textual Commentary on the Greek New Testament* (2d ed.; Stuttgart: Deutsche Bibelgesellschaft and United Bible Societies, 1994), 475.

5. BAGD, ad loc. The German editions of Bauer, *Wörterbuch* (Berlin: Töpelmann) all have the same statement: 1928[2], col. 592; 1937[3], col. 632; 1952[4], col. 689; 1958[5], col. 751; and 1988[6], pp. 770–71. The

third English edition of BAGD, revised and edited by Frederick William Danker (Chicago: University of Chicago Press, 2000) [now designated BDAG], no longer cites the Lietzmann reference favorably and now presents two [!] lexical entries: Ἰουνία and Ἰουνιᾶς, though the latter concludes: "For the strong possibility that a woman named *Junia* is meant s[ee] prec[eding] entry."

6. James Hope Moulton and William Francis Howard, *A Grammar of New Testament Greek, Vol. II: Accidence and Word-Formation* (Edinburgh: T. & T. Clark, 1920), §63 (p. 155).

7. H. Lietzmann, *An die Römer* (HNT 8; Tübingen: Mohr Siebeck, 1906[1]; 1971[5]), ad loc. It is of more than passing interest that Lietzmann, in his commentary on 1 Corinthians, asserted that Paul, in 11:2–16, unwillingly accepted women speaking, but that in 14:34–35 he revealed his true views (*An die Korinther* [HNT 9; Tübingen: Mohr Siebeck, 1949[4]], ad loc; I have this from Conzelmann, *1 Corinthians*, 246).

8. Among those who offer a general argument, see Elisabeth Schüssler Fiorenza, *In Memory of Her: A Feminist Theological Reconstruction of Christian Origins* (New York: Crossroad, 1983), 179–80; eadem, "Missionaries, Apostles, Coworkers: Romans 16 and the Reconstruction of Women's Early Christian History," *Word and World* 6 (1986) 420–33, esp. 427–31; Schulz, "Romans 16:7: Junia or Junias?" 110; idem, "Junia Reinstated: Her Sisters Still Waiting," *Lutheran Theological Journal* [Australia] 38 (2004) 131–34; Elizabeth A. Castelli, "Romans," in *Searching the Scriptures, Volume Two: A Feminist Commentary*, ed. Elisabeth Schüssler Fiorenza (New York: Crossroad, 1994), 279–80; Beverly Roberts Gaventa, "Romans," in *Women's Bible Commentary*, ed. Carol A. Newsom and Sharon H. Ringe, (Louisville: Westminster John Knox, 1992), 410; R. T. France, "From Romans to the Real World: Biblical Principles and Cultural Change in Relation to Homosexuality and the Ministry of Women," in *Romans and the People of God: Essays in Honor of Gordon D. Fee*, ed. Sven K. Soderlund and N. T. Wright (Grand Rapids: Eerdmans, 1999), 240–42; Heiki Omerzu, *Der Prozeß der Paulus: Eine exegetische und rechtshistorische Untersuchung der Apostelgeschichte* (BZNW 115; Berlin: de Gruyter, 2002), 323 n. 66; Steven Croft, "Text Messages: The Ministry of Women and Romans 16," *Anvil* 21 (2004) 87–94, esp. 90. See also the following two notes.

9. On these matters, see Joseph Fitzmyer, *Romans* (AB 33; New York: Doubleday, 1993), 734–42; and Peter Lampe, "Roman Christians of Romans 16," in *The Romans Debate*, ed. Karl P. Donfried (Peabody, Mass.: Hendrickson, 1991), 219–24.

10. Luise Schottroff, *Let the Oppressed Go Free: Feminine Perspectives on the New Testament* (Louisville: Westminster John Knox, 1993),

36–38, 106–8; David M. Scholar, "Paul's Women Coworkers in Ministry," in *Theology, News and Notes* (Fuller Theological Seminary) 42 (no. 1, March, 1995) 20–22. For extensive information on the names in Romans 16, see Peter Lampe, *From Paul to Valentinus: Christians at Rome in the First Two Centuries*, trans. Michael Steinhauser, ed. Marshall D. Johnson (Minneapolis: Fortress Press, 2003), 153–83.

11. Or better, "a married couple," in acknowledgment of Elisabeth Schüssler Fiorenza's pertinent point about early Christian "missionary pairs": "Paul characterizes neither Prisca nor Junia as 'wives.' Their patriarchal status in the household is of no significance. Rather, he greets both women because of their commitment and accomplishments in the work of the gospel" ("Missionaries, Apostles, Coworkers," 431). See also Mary Rose D'Angelo, "Women Partners in the New Testament," *JFSR* 6 (1990) 72–73.

12. Though often it is speculated that Nereus and his sister are the children of Philologus and Julia (e.g., Fitzmyer, *Romans*, 742).

13. C. E. B. Cranfield, *The Epistle to the Romans* (2 vols.; ICC; Edinburgh: T. & T. Clark, 1979; reprint, 1994), 2:788.

14. A. C. Headlam, "Junias (or Junia)," in James Hastings, ed., *A Dictionary of the Bible* (5 vols.; Edinburgh: T. & T. Clark, 1899), 2:825.

15. William Sanday and Arthur C. Headlam, *A Critical and Exegetical Commentary on the Epistle to the Romans* (ICC; Edinburgh: T. & T. Clark, 1895; 1902⁵), 422–23. Cf. a more recent case: Paul K. Jewett acknowledged that the name could be either Junias or Junia but stated that if the text was read as Junia "then the term 'apostles' must be understood loosely of all those sent forth in Christ's name. . . . Even given this looser sense, one wonders if a woman would have been called an 'apostle' in her own right in New Testament times." Not surprisingly, he favored Junias (Jewett, *The Ordination of Women: An Essay on the Office of Christian Ministry* [Grand Rapids: Eerdmans, 1980], 71).

16. Bernhard Weiss, *Die paulinischen Briefe im berichtigten Text mit kurzer Erläuterung* (Leipzig: Hinrichs, 1896), 124; 1902², 127–28.

17. Thomas Walter Manson, "Romans," *Peake's Commentary on the Bible*, ed. Matthew Black and Harold Henry Rowley (Middlesex, UK: Nelson, 1962), 953.

18. Ernst Käsemann, *Commentary on Romans* (Grand Rapids: Eerdmans, 1980), 414. Cf. Rudolf Schnackenburg, "Apostles before and during Paul's Time," in *Apostolic History and the Gospel: Biblical and Historical Essays Presented to F. F. Bruce on His Sixtieth Birthday*, ed. W. Ward Gasque and Ralph P. Martin (Grand Rapids: Eerdmans, 1970),

293–94. To some extent, the reverse has begun to happen; e.g., Stanley K. Stowers, *A Rereading of Romans: Justice, Jews, and Gentiles* (New Haven: Yale University Press, 1994), 75, referred, without comment, to "Andronicus and Junia, whom Paul designates 'notable among the apostles (16:7).'"

19. Otto Michel, *Der Brief an die Römer* (KEK; Göttingen: Vandenhoeck & Ruprecht, 1955[1]; 1978[5]), 475.

20. Manfred Hauke, *Women in the Priesthood? A Systematic Analysis in the Light of the Order of Creation and Redemption* (San Francisco: Ignatius, 1988), 359.

21. Bernadette J. Brooten, "'Junia . . . Outstanding among the Apostles' (Romans 16:7)," in *Women Priests: A Catholic Commentary on the Vatican Declaration*, ed. L. S. and A. Swidler (New York: Paulist, 1977), 142.

22. Castelli, "Romans," 279.

9. Junia/Junias in Greek New Testaments and Their Influence on Exegesis

1. Linda Belleville, "'Ιουνιαν . . . ἐπίσημοι ἐν τοῖς ἀποστόλοις: A Re-examination of Romans 16.7 in Light of Primary Source Materials," *NTS* 51 (2005) 236–237, presents summary information on a number of European translations of the New Testament showing, in general, that the masculine Junias appeared consistently from the mid-1940s to the mid-1970s, with the feminine Junia "consistently" found earlier, and then reappearing in numerous cases from the mid-1970s to the present. However, 237 n.24, from Luther's time forward German versions were "consistently masculine," along with the Dutch and French.

2. Weymouth, *Resultant Greek Testament*, p. xi. Peter Arzt, "Iunia oder Iunias? Zum textkritischen Hintergrund von Röm 16,7," in *Liebe zum Wort: Beiträge zur klassischen und biblischen Philologie*, ed. F. V. Reiterer and P. Eder (Salzburg: Otto Müller, 1993), 95–96, provides some additional items, unavailable to me, that read Ἰουνίαν: Complutensian Polyglot, 1514–1522; Bengel, 1734; Vogels, 1920. He notes that the editions of Daniel Mace, 1729, and Edward Harwood, 1776, leave the name unaccented, though the former opts for Junias in his translation.

3. Henry Alford, *The Greek New Testament, with a Critically Revised Text; . . . and a Critical and Exegetical Commentary* (4 vols.; London: Rivingtons; Cambridge: Deighton, Bell, 1844–1857; 1877[7]), 2:467.

4. I say "presumably the feminine Junia," or, in Tables 1 and 2, "Ἰουνίαν (Presumed Feminine)" because someone may still wish to appeal to the theory that Ἰουνίαν, so accented, represents a masculine

noun whose nominative form is Ἰουνίας, but the discussion above, including the evidence from John Thorley, makes it extremely unlikely that Ἰουνίας can be a male name (see 23–31, 39, 42–44, above).

10. Junia/Junias in English Translations

1. J. B. Lightfoot, *On a Fresh Revision of the English New Testament* (London: Macmillan, 1871¹, 1891³), 179.

2. James D. G. Dunn, *Romans 9–16*, WBC 38 (Dallas: Word, 1988), 894.

3. Ray R. Schulz, "Junia Reinstated: Her Sisters Still Waiting," *Lutheran Theological Journal* [Australia] 38 (2004) 134; see the full article, 129–43, on a range of issues addressed to clergy. Also his "Romans 16:7: Junia or Junias?" *ExpT* 98 (1986/87) 108–10 [but see chap. 5, note 15, above]. Schulz was inspired to investigate these issues when learning (from Major D. Clarke, "Female Ministry in the Salvation Army," *ExpT* 95 (1983/84) 232–35) that William Booth, founder of the Salvation Army (1870) opened all positions equally to men and women, a view traceable to a pamphlet by Booth's spouse, Catherine, *Women's Ministry: Woman's Right to Preach the Gospel* (1859), in which she invoked the female apostle, Junia: Schultz, "Junia Reinstated," 134; cf. idem, "Romans 16:7: Junia or Junias?" 108. In 2000, when presenting a paper on Junia to a meeting of New Testament faculty from member institutions of the Boston Theological Institute—and learning that one of them still used a 1960s N-A (!)—I asserted that unless they had a 1998 or later printing of N-A²⁷ or UBS⁴, they did not possess the Greek text of the New Testament!

11. Andronicus and Junia as "Outstanding among the Apostles"

1. William Sanday and Arthur C. Headlam, *A Critical and Exegetical Commentary on the Epistle to the Romans* (ICC; Edinburgh: T. & T. Clark, 1895; 1902⁵), 423. The same view was defended, for example, in commentaries by M.-J. Lagrange, C. E. B. Cranfield, J. D. G. Dunn, J. A. Fitzmyer, and Douglas Moo, and by others, though all of them favor "Junia" rather than "Junias." Also, Stefan Schreiber, "Arbeit mit der Gemeinde (Röm 16.6, 12): Zur versunkenen Möglichkeit der Gemeindeleitung durch Frauen," *NTS* 46 (2000) 212–14, takes Junia to be an apostle and Andronicus and Junia to be "outstanding among the apostles," as does Peter Richardson, "From Apostles to Virgins: Romans 16 and the Roles of Women in the Early Church," *TJT* 2 (1986) 238–39.

2. Among many treatments, see Ben Witherington III, *Women in the Earliest Churches* (SNTSMS 59; Cambridge: Cambridge University Press, 1988), 115–16; similarly, his *Women and the Genesis of Christianity* (Cambridge: Cambridge University Press, 1990), 187–90.

3. For a quick summary, see Barbara E. Reid, O.P., "Puzzling Passages," *Bible Today* 39 (2001) 244–45, who further enlarges the list of early apostles. Joseph A. Fitzmyer, *Romans* (AB 33; New York: Doubleday, 1993), 739, notes that Paul distinguishes between "the Twelve" and *apostoloi* (1 Cor 15:5, 7), and that "the title 'apostle' was given in the early church not only to the Twelve, but to others as well who were understood as commissioned itinerant evangelists." Also, see now the succinct and insightful discussion in Richard Bauckham, *Gospel Women: Studies of the Named Women in the Gospels* (Grand Rapids: Eerdmans, 2002), 179–80, e.g., that Paul is not using here a "nontechnical sense" of "apostle," as in "apostles of the churches" (2 Cor 8:23; Phil 2:25), but he refers to apostles of Christ, like himself, who have been commissioned by the risen Christ, and who, together with the "Twelve" of the Synoptics, form a larger group. Useful, too, is Wolfgang A. Bienert's "Picture of the Apostle in Early Christian Tradition," *New Testament Apocrypha*, ed. Wilhelm Schneemelcher (2 vols.; rev. ed.; Eng. trans. ed. by R. McL. Wilson; Louisville: Westminster John Knox, 1991–92), 2:5–27, esp. 10–14; 17–18; 24–25.

4. Elisabeth Schüssler Fiorenza, "Missionaries, Apostles, Coworkers: Romans 16 and the Reconstruction of Women's Early Christian History," *Word and World* 6 (1986) 431.

5. Cf. ibid.

6. "Another" designates (for Brock) Mary Magdalene (as in the title of her book: see the following note).

7. Ann Graham Brock, *Mary Magdalene, the First Apostle: The Struggle for Authority* (HTS 51; Cambridge: Harvard University Press, 2003), 147. "Apostleship" is discussed throughout the volume.

8. Sanday and Headlam, *Romans*, 423. Cf. the article on "Junias" in *ISBE* (rev. ed., 1979–1988), 2:1165–66.

9. Sanday and Headlam, *Romans*, 423.

10. Bruce M. Metzger, *A Textual Commentary on the Greek New Testament* (2d ed.; Stuttgart: Deutsche Bibelgesellschaft and United Bible Societies, 1994), 475.

11. Ernst Käsemann, *Commentary on Romans* (Grand Rapids: Eerdmans, 1980), 414; cf. Rudolf Schnackenburg, "Apostles before and during Paul's Time," in *Apostolic History and the Gospel*, ed. W. Ward Gasque and Ralph P. Martin (Grand Rapids: Eerdmans, 1970), 293–94.

12. Michael H. Burer and Daniel B. Wallace, "Was Junia Really an Apostle? A Re-examination of Rom 16.7," *NTS* 47 (2001) 76–91; cf. the brief article by Wallace on "Innovations in Text and Translation of the NET Bible, New Testament," *BT* (Technical Papers) 52 (2001) 343–44.

13. Burer and Wallace, "Was Junia Really an Apostle?" 76.

14. Ibid., 85–86.

15. Richard Bauckham, *Gospel Women: Studies of the Named Women in the Gospels* (Grand Rapids: Eerdmans, 2002), 178, questions their distinction between "personal" and "impersonal" and the priority given to the former, for there appears to be no grammatical difference between the two.

16. Burer and Wallace, "Was Junia Really an Apostle?" 84.

17. Ibid.

18. Richard Bauckham, *Gospel Women*, 165–80.

19. Linda Belleville, "Ἰουνιαν . . . ἐπίσημοι ἐν τοῖς ἀποστόλοις: A Re-examination of Romans 16.7 in Light of Primary Source Materials," *NTS* 51 (2005) 231–49.

20. Burer and Wallace, "Was Junia Really an Apostle?" 87.

21. Bauckham, *Gospel Women*, 175–76: Burer and Wallace fail to report the ἐν before ἐπισήμῳ and the latter is a substantive, not an adjective (as they explicitly call it), which is required for a parallel. Hence, says Bauckham, "this passage must be dropped from the evidence altogether," as must seven (!) more of their meager examples (including 1 Macc 11:37; 14:48) (176).

22. Burer and Wallace, "Was Junia Really an Apostle?" 87. Bauckham, 176, dismissed two of the Oxyrhynchus examples (see preceding note).

23. Burer and Wallace, "Was Junia Really an Apostle?" 88. A similarly biased translation is given on 88 n. 54.

24. My translation, supplemented by that of Belleville (245).

25. Burer and Wallace, "Was Junia Really an Apostle?" 88 n. 53.

26. Belleville, "A Re-examination of Romans 16.7," 245.

27. Burer and Wallace, "Was Junia Really an Apostle?" 88–89.

28. Ibid., 89 n. 63.

29. Ibid., 89.

30. Bauckham, *Gospel Women*, 176 n. 290, nor could I find it in the Loeb edition of Lucian's *de Morte Peregrini* (*The Passing of Peregrinus*), 6.1 or 22.2, even after searching the entire text.

31. Belleville, "A Re-examination of Romans 16.7," 246. I reproduce her texts.

32. Bauckham, *Gospel Women*, 174.

33. Belleville, "A Re-examination of Romans 16.7," 243.

34. Ibid., 244.

35. Ibid., 245. See the full discussion, 244–48. (There may be some doubt about the Philo example.)

36. Bauckham, *Gospel Women*, 178–79. Cf. Belleville, "A Re-examination of Romans 16.7," 247.

37. Burer and Wallace, "Was Junia Really an Apostle?" 88.

38. Ibid., 86.

39. Ibid., 90.

40. Ibid. Burer and Wallace, "Was Junia Really an Apostle?" 90 n. 67, quote a personal letter from C. F. D. Moule that offers support for their view while expressing surprise and asking, "Why, on the 'exclusive' view ["well known to the apostles"], should the *apostles* be mentioned? Why not the community at large, or *all* the Christian communities . . . ?" To my mind, that remains a pertinent question.

Conclusion: There Was an Apostle Junia

1. Michael H. Burer and Daniel B. Wallace, "Was Junia Really an Apostle? A Re-examination of Rom 16.7," *NTS* 47 (2001) 76 n. 2; 77 n. 6. Richard Bauckham, *Gospel Women: Studies of the Named Women in the Gospels* (Grand Rapids: Eerdmans, 2002), 179, calls it a "major error" for Burer and Wallace to dismiss the patristic evidence.

2. Καίτοι καὶ τὸ ἀποστόλους εἶναι μέγα, τὸ δὲ καὶ ἐν τούτοις ἐπισήμους εἶναι ἐννόησον ἡλίκον ἐγκώμιον. Ἐπίσημοι δὲ ἦσαν ἀπὸ τῶν ἔργων, ἀπὸ τῶν κατορθωμάτων. Βαβαί, πόση τῆς γυναικὸς ταύτης ἡ φιλοσοφία, ὡς καὶ τῆς τῶν ἀποστόλων ἀξιωθῆναι προσηγορίας [*In ep. ad Romanos* 31.2 (PG 60:669–70)]. Peter Arzt, "Iunia oder Iunias? Zum textkritischen Hintergrund von Röm 16,7" in *Liebe zum Wort: Beiträge zur klassischen und biblischen Philologie*, ed. F. V. Reiterer and P. Eder (Salzburg: Otto Müller, 1993), 93, notes that this comment of Chrysostom is quoted fairly closely by minuscules 1962 (eleventh century), 1942 (twelfth), and 1678 (fourteenth), and more freely by 1908 (eleventh).

3. James Denney, *St. Paul's Epistle to the Romans*, The Expositor's Greek Testament (Grand Rapids: Eerdmans, 1956 [original, 5 vols., 1897–1910]), ad loc. (italics added). Cf. Bauckham, *Gospel Women*, 179.

4. Manfred Hauke, *Women in the Priesthood? A Systematic Analysis in the Light of the Order of Creation and Redemption* (San Francisco: Ignatius, 1988), 359.

BIBLIOGRAPHY

⊞ ⊞ ⊞

Note: Editions of the Greek New Testament and English translations are included here only if discussed in the text of the volume. The remaining items in the three tables may be identified by consulting, e.g., the following:

Schaff, Philip. *A Companion to the Greek Testament and the English Version.* New York and London: Harper, 1903. See pp. 497–524 for a list of Greek New Testaments, by Isaac H. Hall, from 1514 to 1887.

Darlow, T. H., and H. F. Moule, *Historical Catalogue of the Printed Editions of Holy Scripture in the Library of the British and Foreign Bible Society.* 2 vols. in 4. London: Bible House, 1903–1911. See vol. 1 for English and vol. 2.3 for Greek Bibles.

Herbert, A. S. *Historical Catalogue of the Printed Editions of the English Bible 1525–1961.* Rev. and exp. from Darlow and Moule. London: British and Foreign Bible Society; New York: American Bible Society, 1968.

Hills, Margaret T. *The English Bible in America: A Bibliography of Editions of the Bible and the New Testament Published in America 1777–1957.* New York: American Bible Society and New York Public Library, 1961.

Sheeley, Steven M., and Robert N. Nash Jr. *The Bible in English Translation: An Essential Guide.* Nashville: Abingdon, 1997. See pp. 109–14 for a selected list of English versions through 1996.

Aland and Aland (below). *The Text of the New Testament,* 1989. See pp. 3–47 for a discussion of Greek New Testament editions through N-A^{26} and UBS^4.

⊞ ⊞ ⊞

Aland, Barbara, Kurt Aland, Johannes Karavidopoulos, Carlo M. [Cardinal] Martini, and Bruce M. Metzger, eds. *Novum Testamentum Graece post Eberhard et Erwin Nestle.* 27th ed., 8th corrected printing, with Papyri 99–116. Stuttgart: Deutsche Bibelgesellschaft, 2001. (= Nestle-Aland^{27})

————, eds. *The Greek New Testament*. 4th rev. ed., 5th printing, with Papyri 98–116. Stuttgart: Deutsche Bibelgesellschaft and United Bible Societies, 2001. (= UBSGNT⁴ or UBS⁴)

Aland, Kurt. *Vollständige Konkordanz zum griechischen Neuen Testament*. 2 vols. ANTF 4. Berlin: de Gruyter, 1975–1983.

————, ed. *Text und Textwert der griechischen Handschriften des Neuen Testaments II: Die paulinischen Briefe, Band 1: Allgemeines, Römerbrief und Ergänzungsliste*. Berlin: de Gruyter, 1991.

Aland, Kurt, and Barbara Aland. *The Text of the New Testament: An Introduction to the Critical Editions and to the Theory and Practice of Modern Textual Criticism*. 2d ed. Grand Rapids: Eerdmans; Leiden: Brill, 1989.

Aland, Kurt, and Barbara Aland, eds. *Griechisch-deutsches Wörterbuch*. Berlin: de Gruyter, 1988. This is the latest German edition of Walter Bauer's lexicon.

Alford, Henry. *The Greek New Testament, with a Critically Revised Text; . . . and a Critical and Exegetical Commentary*. 4 vols. London: Rivingtons; Cambridge: Deighton, Bell, 1844–1857; 1877⁷.

Allison, Robert W. "Let Women Be Silent in the Churches (1 Cor. 14.33b-36): What Did Paul Really Say, and What Did It Mean?" *JSNT* 32 (1988) 27–60.

Arichea, Daniel C. "The Silence of Women in the Church: Theology and Translation in 1 Corinthians 14.33b-36." *BT* (Technical Papers) 46 (1995) 101–12.

Arzt, Peter. "Iunia oder Iunias? Zum textkritischen Hintergrund von Röm 16,7." In *Liebe zum Wort: Beiträge zur klassischen und biblischen Philologie, P. Ludger Bernhard OSB zum 80. Geburtstag dargebracht von Kollegen und Schülern*, ed. F. V. Reiterer and P. Eder, 83–102. Salzburg: Otto Müller, 1993.

Bassler, Jouette M. "1 Corinthians." In *Women's Bible Commentary, Expanded Edition*, ed. Carol A. Newsom and Sharon H. Ringe, ad loc. Louisville: Westminster John Knox, 1998.

Bauckham, Richard. *Gospel Women: Studies of the Named Women in the Gospels*. Grand Rapids: Eerdmans, 2002.

Bauer, Walter. *Griechisch-deutsches Wörterbuch zu den Schriften des Neuen Testaments und der übrigen urchristlichen Literatur*. Berlin, 1928 = 2d ed. of Preuschen; 3d ed., 1937; 4th ed., 1949–1952; 5th ed., 1957–1958. See Aland and Aland for 6th ed., 1988.

Belleville, Linda. "Ἰουνιαν . . . ἐπίσημοι ἐν τοῖς ἀποστόλοις: A Reexamination of Romans 16.7 in Light of Primary Source Materials." *NTS* 51 (2005) 231–49.

Bienert, Wolfgang A. "Picture of the Apostle in Early Christian Tradition." In *New Testament Apocrypha*, ed. Wilhelm Schneemelcher, 2:5–27. Rev. ed. Eng. trans. ed. R. McL. Wilson. Louisville: Westminster John Knox, 1991–92.

Blass, Friedrich. *Grammatik des neutestamentlichen Griechisch*. Göttingen, 1896. Rev. by Albert Debrunner, 1913⁴–1954⁹; rev. by Friedrich Rehkopf, 1976.¹⁴ English trans.: Henry St. John Thackeray, *Grammar of New Testament Greek*. London: Macmillan, 1898.

Brock, Ann Graham. *Mary Magdalene, the First Apostle: The Struggle for Authority*. HTS 51. Cambridge: Harvard University Press, 2003.

Brooten, Bernadette J. "'Junia . . . Outstanding among the Apostles' (Romans 16:7)." In *Women Priests: A Catholic Commentary on the Vatican Declaration*, ed. L. S. and A. Swidler, 148–51. New York: Paulist, 1977. German trans.: "'Junia . . . Hervorragend unter den Aposteln' (Röm 16,7)." In *Frauenbefreiung: Biblische und theologische Argumente*, ed. Elisabeth Moltmann-Wendel, 148–51. Munich: Chr. Kaiser, 1978; 1982³.

Bryce, David W. "'As in All the Churches of the Saints': A Text-Critical Study of 1 Corinthians 14:34-35." *Lutheran Theological Journal* [Australia] 31 (1997) 31–39. Response to Lockwood.

Burer, Michael H., and Daniel B. Wallace. "Was Junia Really an Apostle? A Reexamination of Rom 16.7." *NTS* 47 (2001) 76–91.

Carson, Donald A. "'Silent in the Churches': On the Role of Women in 1 Corinthians 14:33b-36." In *Recovering Biblical Manhood and Womanhood: A Response to Evangelical Feminism*, ed. J. Piper and W. Grudem, 140–53. Wheaton, Ill.: Crossway, 1991.

Castelli, Elizabeth A. "Romans." In *Searching the Scriptures, Volume Two: A Feminist Commentary*, ed. Elisabeth Schüssler Fiorenza, 272–300. New York: Crossroad, 1994.

Cervin, Richard S. "A Note regarding the Name 'Junia(s)' in Romans 16.7." *NTS* 40 (1994) 464–70.

Clarke, [Major] Douglas. "Female Ministry in the Salvation Army." *ExpT* 95 (1983/84) 232–35.

Clarke, Graham. "'As in all the Churches of the Saints.'" *BT* 52 (2001) 144–47.

Conzelmann, Hans. *1 Corinthians: A Commentary on the First Epistle to the Corinthians*. Hermeneia. Philadelphia: Fortress Press, 1975.

Cranfield, Charles Ernest Burland. *The Epistle to the Romans*. 2 vols. ICC. Edinburgh: T. & T. Clark, 1979; reprint, 1994.

Croft, Steven. "Text Messages: The Ministry of Women and Romans 16." *Anvil* 21 (2004) 87–94.

Croy, N. Clayton. "Where the Gospel Text Begins: A Non-Theological Interpretation of Mark 1:1." *NovT* 43 (2001) 105–27.

Crüsemann, Marlene. "Irredeemably Hostile to Women: Anti-Jewish Elements in the Exegesis of the Dispute about Women's Right to Speak (1 Cor. 14.34–35)." *JSNT* 79 (2000) 19–36.

D'Angelo, Mary Rose. "Women Partners in the New Testament." *JFSR* 6 (1990) 65–86.

Delobel, Joël. "Textual Criticism and Exegesis: Siamese Twins?" In *New Testament Textual Criticism, Exegesis, and Early Church History: A Discussion of Methods*, ed. Barbara Aland and Joël Delobel, 98–117. Kampen: Kok Pharos, 1994.

————. "The Text of Luke-Acts: A Confrontation of Recent Theories." In *The Unity of Luke-Acts*, ed. J. Verheyden, 83–107. BETL 142. Leuven: Peeters and Leuven University Press, 1999.

Denney, James. *St. Paul's Epistle to the Romans*. In *The Expositor's Greek Testament*, ed. W. R. Nicoll, 2.555–725. 5 vols. London: Hodder and Stoughton, 1897–1910; reprint, Grand Rapids: Eerdmans, 1956.

Donfried, Karl Paul, ed. *The Romans Debate*. Rev. and exp. ed. Peabody, Mass.: Hendrickson, 1991.

————. "A Short Note on Romans 16." In *The Romans Debate*, ed. K. P. Donfried, 44–52. Peabody, Mass.: Hendrickson, 1991.

Dunn, James D. G. *Romans 9–16*. WBC 38. Dallas: Word, 1988.

du Toit, Andrie. "Die swyggebod van 1 Korintiërs 14:34–35 weer eens onder die loep." *Hervormde Teologiese Studies* 57 (2001) 172–86.

Ehrman, Bart D. *The Orthodox Corruption of Scripture: The Effect of Early Christological Controversies on the Text of the New Testament.* New York: Oxford University Press, 1993.

————. "The Text as Window: New Testament Manuscripts and the Social History of Early Christianity." In *The Text of the New Testament in Contemporary Research: Essays on the* Status Quaestionis, ed. Bart D. Ehrman and Michael W. Holmes, 361–79. SD 46. Grand Rapids: Eerdmans, 1995.

Elliott, James Keith. "Mark 1.1–3: A Later Addition to the Gospel?" *NTS* 46 (2000) 584–88.

Ellis, Arthur Ayres. *Bentleii Critica Sacra*. Cambridge: Deighton, Bell, 1862.

Ellis, Edward Earle. "The Silenced Wives of Corinth (1 Cor. 14: 34–5)." In *New Testament Textual Criticism, Its Significance for Exegesis: Essays in Honour of Bruce M. Metzger*, ed. E. J. Epp and Gordon D. Fee, 213–20. Oxford: Clarendon, 1981.

Epp, Eldon Jay. *The Theological Tendency of Codex Bezae Cantabrigiensis in Acts.* SNTSMS 3. Cambridge: Cambridge University Press, 1966.

———. "The Multivalence of the Term 'Original Text' in New Testament Textual Criticism." *HTR* 92 (1999) 245–81.

———. "Issues in New Testament Textual Criticism: Moving from the Nineteenth to the Twenty-First Century." In *Rethinking New Testament Textual Criticism*, ed. David Alan Black, 17–76. Grand Rapids: Baker Academic, 2002.

———. "Text-Critical, Exegetical, and Socio-Cultural Factors Affecting the Junia/Junias Variation in Romans 16,7," *Textual Criticism and Exegesis: Festschrift J. Delobel*, ed. A. Denaux, 227–91. BETL 161. Leuven: Leuven University Press and Peeters, 2002.

Fàbrega, Valentin. "War Junia(s), der hervorragende Apostel (Rom. 16,7), eine Frau?" *JAC* 27/28 (1984/1985) 47–64.

Fee, Gordon Donald. *The First Epistle to the Corinthians.* NICNT. Grand Rapids: Eerdmans, 1987.

———. *God's Empowering Presence: The Holy Spirit in the Letters of Paul.* Peabody, Mass.: Hendrickson, 1994.

Fischer, Bonafatius, OSB, ed. *Novae Concordantiae Bibliorum Sacrorum iuxta vulgatam versionem critice editam.* 5 vols. Stuttgart: Frommann-Holzboog, 1977.

Fitzer, Gottfried. *Das Weib schweige in der Gemeinde: Über den unpaulinischen Charakter der mulier-taceat Verse in 1. Korinther 14.* Theologische Existenz Heute 10. Munich: Chr. Kaiser, 1963.

Fitzmyer, Joseph A. *Romans.* AB 33. New York: Doubleday, 1993.

Flanagan, Neal M., and Edwina Hunter Snyder, "Did Paul Put Down Women in 1 Cor 14:34–36?" *BTB* 11 (1981) 10–12.

France, R. T. "From Romans to the Real World: Biblical Principles and Cultural Change in Relation to Homosexuality and the Ministry of Women." In *Romans and the People of God: Essays in Honor of Gordon D. Fee on the Occasion of His Sixty-fifth Birthday*, ed. Sven K. Soderlund and N. T. Wright, 234–53. Grand Rapids: Eerdmans, 1999.

Gamble, Harry Y. *The Textual History of the Letter to the Romans: A Study in Textual and Literary Criticism.* SD 42. Grand Rapids: Eerdmans, 1977.

Gaventa, Beverly Roberts. "Romans." In *Women's Bible Commentary, Expanded Edition*, ed. Carol A. Newsom and Sharon H. Ringe, ad loc. Louisville: Westminster John Knox, 1998.

Gingrich, Felix Wilbur. "Junias/Junia," *IDB* 2:1026–27.

———, and Frederick William Danker. *Shorter Lexicon of the Greek New Testament.* 2d ed. Chicago: University of Chicago Press, 1983.

Gourgues, Michel. "Who Is Misogynist: Paul or Certain Corinthians? Note on 1 Corinthians 14:33b-36." In *Women Also Journeyed with Him: Feminist Perspectives on the Bible*, ed. Gérald Caron et al., 117–24. Collegeville, Minn.: Liturgical, 2000.

Greenslade, Stanley Lawrence, ed. *The West from the Reformation to the Present Day.* The Cambridge History of the Bible 3. Cambridge: Cambridge University Press, 1963.

Grimm, Karl Ludwig Wilibald. *Lexicon Graeco-Latinum in libros Novi Testamenti.* Leipzig: Arnold, 1862, 1879[2].

Hammond Bammel, Caroline P. *Der Römerbrieftext des Rufin und seine Origenes-Übersetzung.* Vetus Latina, Aus der Geshichte der lateinischen Bibel 10. Freiburg: Herder, 1985.

———. *Der Römerbriefkommentar des Origenes: Kritische Ausgabe der Übersetzung Rufins.* 3 vols. Vetus Latina, Aus der Geshichte der lateinischen Bibel 16, 33, 34. Freiburg: Herder, 1990, 1997, 1998.

Hauke, Manfred. *Women in the Priesthood? A Systematic Analysis in the Light of the Order of Creation and Redemption.* San Francisco: Ignatius, 1988.

Hayes, Richard B. *First Corinthians.* Interpretation. Louisville: John Knox, 1997. On 1 Cor 14:34–35, see pp. 245–49.

Headlam, Arthur Cayley. "Junias (or Junia)." In *A Dictionary of the Bible*, ed. James Hastings, 2:825. 5 vols. Edinburgh: T. & T. Clark, 1899.

Heine, Susanne. *Women and Early Christianity: A Reappraisal.* Trans. John Bowden. Minneapolis: Augsburg, 1988.

Holmes, Michael W. "Reasoned Eclecticism in New Testament Textual Criticism." In *The Text of the New Testament in Contemporary Research: Essays on the Status Quaestionis*, ed. Bart D. Ehrman and Michael W. Holmes, 336–60. SD 46. Grand Rapids: Eerdmans, 1995.

Hort, Fenton John Anthony. *Prolegomena to St Paul's Epistles to the Romans and the Ephesians.* London: Macmillan, 1895.

Jewett, Paul K. *The Ordination of Women: An Essay on the Office of Christian Ministry.* Grand Rapids: Eerdmans, 1980.

Jordan, Clarence. *Cotton Patch Version of Paul's Epistles.* New York: Association, 1968.

Karris, Robert J. "Women in the Pauline Assembly: To Prophesy but Not to Speak?" In *Women Priests: A Catholic Commentary on the Vatican Declaration*, ed. Leonard S. and Arlene Swidler, 205–8. New York: Paulist, 1977.

Käsemann, Ernst. *Commentary on Romans.* Grand Rapids: Eerdmans, 1980.

Keener, Craig S. *Paul, Women and Wives: Marriage and Women's Ministry in the Letters of Paul*. Peabody, Mass.: Hendrickson, 1992. On 1 Cor 14:34–35, see 70–100.

King, Karen Leigh. "Why All the Controversy? Mary in the *Gospel of Mary*." In *Which Mary? The Marys of Early Christian Tradition*, ed. F. Stanley Jones, 53–74. SBLSymS 19. Atlanta: Society of Biblical Literature, 2002.

———. *The Gospel of Mary of Magdala: Jesus and the First Woman Apostle*. Santa Rosa, Calif.: Polebridge, 2003.

Kunst, Hermann, ed. *Bericht der Hermann Kunst-Stiftung zur Förderung der neutestamentlichen Textforschung für die Jahre 1995 bis 1998*. Münster: Hermann Kunst-Stiftung, 1998.

Lagrange, Marie-Josèphe. *Saint Paul: Épître aux Romains*. Ebib. Paris: Gabalda, 1914, 1931[4]; repr. 1950.

Lampe, Peter. "Iunia/Iunias: Sklavenherkunft im Kreise der vorpaulinischen Apostel (Röm 16,7)." *ZNW* 76 (1985) 132–34.

———. "The Roman Christians of Romans 16." In *The Romans Debate*, ed. Karl P. Donfried, 219–24. Peabody, Mass.: Hendrickson, 1991.

———. "Junias." *ABD* 3:1127.

———. *From Paul to Valentinus: Christians at Rome in the First Two Centuries*. Trans. Michael Steinhauser. Ed. Marshall D. Johnson. Minneapolis: Fortress Press, 2003.

Legg, Stanley Charles Edmund, ed. *Nouum Testamentum graece secundum textum Westcotto-Hortianum: Euangelium secundum Marcum*. Oxford: Clarendon, 1935.

———. *Nouum Testamentum graece secundum textum Westcotto-Hortianum: Euangelium secundum Matthaeum*. Oxford: Clarendon, 1940.

Lietzmann, Hans. *An die Korinther*. HNT 9. Tübingen: Mohr Siebeck, 1949[4].

———. *An die Römer*. HNT 8. Tübingen: Mohr Siebeck, 1906[1]; 1971[5].

Lightfoot, Joseph Barber. *On a Fresh Revision of the English New Testament*. London: Macmillan, 1871[1], 1891[3].

Lindboe, Inger Marie. *Women in the New Testament: A Select Bibliography*. Bibliography Series 1. Oslo: University of Oslo, Faculty of Theology, 1990.

Locke, John. *A Paraphrase and Notes on the Epistles of St Paul to the Galatians, 1 and 2 Corinthians, Romans, Ephesians*. Ed. Arthur W. Wainwright. 2 vols. Oxford: Clarendon, 1987.

Lockwood, Peter F. "Does 1 Corinthians 14:34–35 Exclude Women from the Pastoral Office?" *Lutheran Theological Journal* [Australia] 30 (1996) 30–38.

Lohfink, Gerhard. "Weibliche Diakone im Neuen Testament." In *Die Frau im Urchristentum*, ed. Gerhard Dautzenberg, H. Merklein, and K. Müller, 320–38. Freiberg: Herder, 1983.

Louw, Johannes P., and Eugene A. Nida, eds. *Greek-English Lexicon of the New Testament Based on Semantic Domains.* 2d ed. 2 vols. New York: United Bible Societies, 1989.

Manson, Thomas Walter. "Romans." In *Peake's Commentary on the Bible*, ed. Matthew Black and Harold Henry Rowley, 940–53. Middlesex, UK: Nelson, 1962.

Metzger, Bruce Manning (for the Editorial Committee). *A Textual Commentary on the Greek New Testament.* 2d ed. Stuttgart: Deutsche Bibelgesellschaft and United Bible Societies, 1994.

Michel, Otto. *Der Brief an die Römer.* KEK. Göttingen: Vandenhoeck & Ruprecht, 1955[1]; 1978[5].

Miller, J. Edward. "Some Observations on the Text-Critical Function of the Umlauts in Vaticanus, with Special Attention to 1 Corinthians 14.34–35." *JSNT* 26 (2003) 217–36.

Moo, Douglas. *Romans 1–8.* Wycliffe Exegetical Commentary. Chicago: Moody, 1991.

Moulton, James Hope, and Wilbert Francis Howard. *A Grammar of New Testament Greek.* Vol. II: *Accidence and Word-Formation.* Edinburgh: T. & T. Clark, 1920.

Moulton, William Fiddian, and Albert Shenington Geden. *A Concordance to the Greek Testament.* Edinburgh: T. & T. Clark, [1]1897, [3]1926.

Murphy-O'Connor, Jerome. "Interpolations in 1 Corinthians." *CBQ* 48 (1986) 81–93.

Newman, Barclay Moon Jr. *A Concise Greek-English Dictionary of the New Testament.* Stuttgart: Deutsche Bibelgesellschaft and United Bible Societies, 1971.

Newman, Barclay Moon Jr., and Eugene Albert Nida. *A Translator's Handbook on Paul's Letter to the Romans.* Helps for Translators 14. London: United Bible Societies, 1973.

Niccum, Curt. "The Voice of the Manuscripts on the Silence of Women: The External Evidence for 1 Cor 14.34–5." *NTS* 43 (1997) 242–55.

Odell-Scott, David W. "Let the Women Speak in Church: An Egalitarian Interpretation of 1 Cor. 14.33b–36." *BTB* 13 (1983) 90–93.

———. "In Defence of an Egalitarian Interpretation of 1 Cor. 14.34–36: A Reply to Murphy-O'Connor's Critique." *BTB* 17 (1987) 100–3.

———. "Editorial Dilemma: The Interpolation of 1 Cor 14:34–35 in the Western Manuscripts of D, G, and 88." *BTB* 30 (2000) 68–74.

Omanson, Roger L. "Who's Who in Romans 16? Identifying Men and Women among the People Paul Sent Greetings To." *BT* 49 (1998) 430–36.

Omerzu, Heike. *Der Prozeß der Paulus: Eine exegetische und rechtshistorische Untersuchung der Apostelgeschichte.* BZNW 115. Berlin: de Gruyter, 2002.

Parker, David C. "A New Oxyrhynchus Papyrus of Revelation: p[115] (P.Oxy. 4499)." *NTS* 46 (2000) 159–74.

———. *The Living Text of the Gospels.* Cambridge: Cambridge University Press, 1997.

Payne, Philip. B. "Fuldensis, Sigla for Variants in Vaticanus, and 1 Cor 14.34–5." *NTS* 41 (1995) 240–62.

———. "Ms. 88 as Evidence for a Text without 1 Cor 14.34–5." *NTS* 44 (1998) 152–58.

———. "The Text-Critical Function of the Umlauts in Vaticanus, with Special Attention to 1 Corinthians 14.34–35: A Response to J. Edward Miller." *JSNT* 27 (2004) 105–12.

Payne, Philip B., and Paul Canart. "The Originality of Text-Critical Symbols in Codex Vaticanus." *NovT* 42 (2000) 105–13.

———. "'Umlauts' Matching the Original Ink of Codex Vaticanus: Do They Mark the Location of Textual Variants?" In *Le manuscrit B de la Bible (Vaticanus gr. 1209): Introduction au fac-similé, Actes du Colloque de Genève (11 juin 2001), Contributions supplémentaires,* ed. Patrick Andrist, 191–214. Lausanne: Èditions du Zèbre, 2004.

Petzer, Jacobus Hendrik. "Reconsidering the Silent Women of Corinth: A Note on 1 Corinthians 14:34–35." *Theologia Evangelica* 26 (1993) 132–38.

Piper, John, and Wayne Grudem. "An Overview of Central Concerns." In *Recovering Biblical Manhood and Womanhood,* ed. J. Piper and W. Grudem, 60–92. Wheaton, Ill.: Crossway, 1991.

———, eds. *Recovering Biblical Manhood and Womanhood: A Response to Evangelical Feminism.* Wheaton, Ill.: Crossway, 1991.

Plisch, U.-K. "Die Apostelin Junia: Das exegetische Problem in Röm 16.7 im Licht von Nestle-Aland[27] und der sahidischen Überlieferung." *NTS* 42 (1996) 477–78.

Preuschen, Erwin. *Vollständiges griechisch-deutsches Handwörterbuch.* Giessen: Töpelmann, 1910.

Reid, Barbara, O.P. "Puzzling Passages." *The Bible Today* 39 (2001) 244–45.

Richardson, Peter. "From Apostles to Virgins: Romans 16 and the Roles of Women in the Early Church." *TJT* 2 (1986) 232–61.

Robertson, Archibald Thomas. *A Grammar of the Greek New Testament in the Light of Historical Research.* Nashville: Broadman, 1934.

Ross, J. M. "Floating Words: Their Significance for Textual Criticism." *NTS* 38 (1992) 153–56.

Sanday, William, and Arthur Cayley Headlam. *A Critical and Exegetical Commentary on the Epistle to the Romans.* ICC. Edinburgh: T. & T. Clark, 1895; 1902⁵.

Schnackenburg, Rudolf. "Apostles before and during Paul's Time." In *Apostolic History and the Gospel: Biblical and Historical Essays Presented to F. F. Bruce on His Sixtieth Birthday*, ed. W. Ward Gasque and Ralph P. Martin, 287–303. Grand Rapids: Eerdmans, 1970.

Schneemelcher, Wilhelm, ed., *New Testament Apocrypha.* Rev. ed. Eng. trans. ed. R. McL. Wilson. Louisville: Westminster John Knox, 1991–92.

Scholar, David Milton. "Paul's Women Coworkers in Ministry." In *Theology, News and Notes* 42 (no. 1, March, 1995), 20–22. Pasadena, Calif.: Fuller Theological Seminary.

Schottroff, Luise. *Let the Oppressed Go Free: Feminine Perspectives on the New Testament.* Louisville: Westminster John Knox, 1993.

Schreiber, Stefen. "Arbeit mit der Gemeinde (Röm 16.6, 12): Zur versunkenen Möglichkeit der Gemeindeleitung durch Frauen." *NTS* 46 (2000) 204–26.

Schreiner, Thomas R. "The Valuable Ministries of Women in the Context of Male Leadership." In *Recovering Biblical Manhood and Womanhood: A Response to Evangelical Feminism*, ed. J. Piper and W. Grudem, 209–24. Wheaton, Ill.: Crossway, 1991.

Schulz, Ray R. "Romans 16:7: Junia or Junias?" *ExpT* 98 (1986/87) 108–10.

———. "Junia Reinstated: Her Sisters Still Waiting." *Lutheran Theological Journal* [Australia] 38 (2004) 129–43.

Schüssler Fiorenza, Elisabeth. *In Memory of Her: A Feminist Theological Reconstruction of Christian Origins.* New York: Crossroad, 1983.

———. "Missionaries, Apostles, Coworkers: Romans 16 and the Reconstruction of Women's Early Christian History." *Word and World* 6 (1986) 420–33.

Sider, Robert D., ed. *New Testament Scholarship, Paraphrases on Romans and Galatians. Collected Works of Erasmus*, vol. 42. Toronto: University of Toronto Press, 1984.

———. *New Testament Scholarship, Annotations on Romans. Collected Works of Erasmus*, vol. 56. Toronto: University of Toronto Press, 1994.

Stapulensis, Jacobus Faber [Jacques LeFèvre d'Étaples]. *S. Pauli episto-
lae XIV ex Vulgata, adiecta intelligentia ex graeco, cum commentariis.*
Facsimile reprint of the Paris edition of 1512. Stuttgart: Frommann-
Holzboog, 1978.

Stowers, Stanley K. *A Rereading of Romans: Justice, Jews, and Gentiles.*
New Haven: Yale University Press, 1994.

Swanson, Reuben J. *New Testament Manuscripts: Variant Readings
arranged in Horizontal Lines against Codex Vaticanus: Romans.*
Wheaton, Ill: Tyndale House, 2001.

Thackeray, Henry St. John. *Grammar of New Testament Greek.* London:
Macmillan, 1898.

Thayer, Joseph Henry. *Greek-English Lexicon of the New Testament,
Being Grimm's Wilke's Clavis Novi Testamenti.* New York: Harper,
1886; cor. ed., 1889.

Thorley, John. "Junia, A Woman Apostle." *NovT* 38 (1996) 18–29.

Walker, William O. "1 Corinthians 11:2–16 and Paul's Views regarding
Women." *JBL* 94 (1975) 94–110.

Wallace, Daniel B. "Innovations in Text and Translation of the NET
Bible, New Testament." *BT* (Technical Papers) 52 (2001) 343–44.

Weiss, Bernhard. *Die paulinischen Briefe im berichtigten Text mit kurzer
Erläuterung.* Leipzig: Hinrichs, 1896; 1902².

Westcott, Brooke Foss, and Fenton John Anthony Hort. *The New Testament in the Original Greek.* 2 vols. London: Macmillan, 1881–82; vol.
2, 2d ed., 1896.

Weymouth, Richard Francis. *The Resultant Greek Testament.* London:
James Clarke, 1886; 1905⁵.

———. *The New Testament in Modern Speech: An Idiomatic Translation into Every-day English from the Text of 'The Resultant Greek Testament.'* London: James Clarke, 1903; 1929⁵.

Wilson, Benjamin. *The Emphatic Diaglott Containing the Original
Greek Text of What Is Commonly Styled the New Testament . . . with
an Interlineary Word for Word English Translation.* Geneva, Ill.: by
the author, 1864; reprint, 1902.

Wire, Antoinette Clark. *The Corinthian Women Prophets: A Reconstruction through Paul's Rhetoric.* Minneapolis: Fortress, 1990. On 1 Cor
14:34–35, see pp. 149–58; 229–32.

———. "1 Corinthians." In *Searching the Scriptures, Volume Two: A
Feminist Commentary,* ed. Elisabeth Schüssler Fiorenza, 153–95.
New York: Crossroad, 1994.

Witherington III, Ben. *Women in the Earliest Churches.* SNTSMS 59.
Cambridge: Cambridge University Press, 1988.

————. *Women and the Genesis of Christianity*. Cambridge: Cambridge University Press, 1990.

Wordsworth, John, and Henry Julian White. *Novum Testamentum Domini nostri Jesu Christi Latine*. 3 vols. Oxford: Clarendon, 1898–1954). Epistles vol., 1913.

Yarbro Collins, Adela. "Establishing the Text: Mark 1:1." In *Texts and Contexts: Biblical Texts in Their Textual and Situational Contexts: Essays in Honor of Lars Hartman*, ed. T. Fornberg and D. Hellholm, 111–27. Oslo: Scandinavian University Press, 1995.

Yeager, Randolph O. *The Renaissance New Testament: Volume Twelve, Romans 9:1–16:27, I Corinthians 1:1—10:33*. Gretna, La.: Pelican, 1983). See pp. 258–59 on Rom 16:7.

INDEX OF PASSAGES

I. BIBLICAL CITATIONS

II. PAPYRI AND INSCRIPTIONS

For New Testament papyri, see Index of New Testament Manuscripts, Versions, Editions, and Modern Translations, below.

III. CLASSICAL AND PATRISTIC CITATIONS

INDEX OF NAMES

I. ANCIENT AND PREMODERN AUTHORS AND PERSONS (TO CA. 1450)

II. MODERN AUTHORS

D'Angelo, Mary Rose, 104 n. 11, 113
Danker, Frederick William, 53–54,
    102 n. 3, 114
Darlow, Thomas Herbert, 110
Dautzenberg, Gerhard, 116
Debrunner, Albert, 25, 40, 55, 58,
    92 n. 5, 98 n. 5, 112
De Jonge, Henk Jan, 85 n. 5
Delobel, Joël, xv, 15, 17, 86 n. 13,
    87 n. 3, 88 n. 6, 89 n. 11, 113
Denaux, Adelbert, 114
Denney, James, 80, 93 n. 10, 109 n.
    3, 113
Dickinson, Rodolphus, 24, 65
Donfried, Karl Paul, 84 nn. 1–2, 91
    n. 2 (chap. 3), 100 n. 20, 102 n.
    7, 103 n. 9, 113, 116
Drusius, Johannes (fl. 1698), 39,
    97 n. 27
Dunn, James D. G., 30–31, 67, 95 n.
    6, 98 n. 8, 106 nn. 2 (chap. 10)
    and 1 (chap. 11), 113
du Toit, Andrie B., 88 n. 9, 113

Eder, Petrus, OSB, 97 n. 29, 99 n. 19,
    100 n. 1, 105 n. 2, 109 n. 2, 111
Ehrman, Bart D., 11, 14, 86 n.12,
    87 nn. 32–33 (chap. 1) and 1
    (chap. 2), 113, 115
Elliott, James Keith, 86 n. 16, 113
Ellis, Arthur Ayres, 97 n. 29, 113
Ellis, E. Earle, 89 n. 10, 113
Erasmus, Desiderius (ca. 1466–
    1536), 23, 27–28, 35–36, 39, 61,
    96 n. 23
Epp, Eldon Jay, x–xiii, 84 n. 1, 85
    nn. 4–7 and 9, 86 nn. 11, 13,
    and 15, 87 nn. 34–35 (chap. 1)
    and 2 (chap. 2), 89 n. 10, 114

Fàbrega, Valentin, 95 nn. 7 and 9,
    114
Fee, Gordon Donald, 16–17, 88 nn.

7–8, 89 n. 10, 90 n. 25, 113–14
Fiorenza, Elisabeth Schüssler: See
    Schüssler Fiorenza
Fischer, Bonifatius, 37, 96 n. 19, 114
Fitzer, Gottfried, 88 n. 9, 114
Fitzmyer, Joseph A., S.J., 30, 32, 50-
    51, 94 n. 1, 95 nn. 8 and 12, 98
    n. 8, 101 n. 6, 103 n. 9, 106 n. 1,
    107 n. 3, 114
Flanagan, Neal M., 89 n. 10, 114
Fornberg, Tord, 86 n. 16, 121
France, Richard Thomas, 103 n.
    8, 114
Funk, Robert Walter, 40

Gamble, Harry Y., 84 n. 2, 85 n. 5,
    114
Gasque, W. Ward, 104 n. 18, 107 n.
    11, 119
Gaventa, Beverly Roberts, xiii, xvi,
    103 n. 8, 114
Geden, Albert Shenington, 26, 93
    n. 13, 117
Gingrich, Felix Wilbur, 53, 58, 102
    n. 3, 114
Goodspeed, Edgar Johnson, 97 n. 30
Gourgues, Michel, 90 n. 25, 115
Greenslade, Stanley Lawrence, 96
    nn. 22–23, 115
Grimm, Karl Ludwig Wilibald, 41,
    92 n. 6, 98 n. 6, 115
Gritsch, Eric W., 95 n. 20,
Grudem, Wayne, 34, 88 n. 8, 95 n.
    10, 98 n. 9, 112, 118–19
Gruytère, Janus (1560–1627), 39

Hammond Bammel, Caroline,
    33–34, 95 n. 7, 115
Harwood, Edward, 105 n. 2
Hastings, James, 104 n. 14, 115
Hauke, Manfred, 58–59, 80–81, 104
    n. 20, 109 n. 4, 115
Hayes, Richard B., 115

⚉ ⚉ ⚉ ⚉ ⚉

INDEX OF GREEK AND LATIN WORDS

INDEX OF NEW TESTAMENT MANU-SCRIPTS, VERSIONS, EDITIONS, AND MODERN TRANSLATIONS

I. GREEK MANUSCRIPTS OF THE NEW TESTAMENT

GREEK PAPYRI

P46 (ca. 200), 17, 46, 94 n. 23

P115 (third/fourth cent.), 7, 86 n. 14

GREEK MAJUSCULES

ℵ (01, Sinaiticus, fourth cent.), 7, 17, 45–46

A (02, Alexandrinus, fifth cent.), 17, 45–46

B (03, Vaticanus, fourth cent.), 7, 17–19, 45–46, 89 n. 13, 90 nn. 14–23, 101 n. 8

C (04, Ephraemi Syri Rescriptus, fifth cent.), 6, 45–46

D (05, Bezae Cantabrigiensis, 400), 7

D^paul (06, Claromontanus, sixth cent.), 17, 45–46, 90 n. 25, 101 n. 8

F^paul (010, Augiensis, ninth cent.), 17, 45–46

G^paul (012, Boernerianus, sixth cent.), 17, 45–46, 90 n. 25

L (020) Codex Angelicus (ninth cent.), 101 n. 8

P (025, Porphyrianus, ninth cent.), 45–46

W (032, Washingtonianus, fifth cent.), 7

Ψ (044, Athous Lavrensis, eighth/ninth cent.), 46, 101 n. 8

0150 (ninth cent.), 46

GREEK MINUSCULES

6 (thirteenth cent.), 46, 100 n. 6

33 (ninth cent.), 46, 51, 95 n. 12, 100 n. 1, 101 n. 8

88 (twelfth cent.), 17, 89 n. 12, 90 nn. 24–25

606 (eleventh cent.), 100 n. 6

1678 (fourteenth cent.), 109 n. 2

1718 (twelfth cent.), 100 n. 6

1739 (tenth cent.), 46, 101 n. 8

1837 (tenth cent.), 100 n. 5

1881 (fourteenth cent.), 46, 101 n. 8

1908 (eleventh cent.), 109 n. 2

1942 (twelfth cent.), 109 n. 2

1962 (eleventh cent.), 46, 109 n. 2

2685 (fifteenth cent.), 100 n. 6

II. VERSIONS OF THE NEW TESTAMENT

III. EDITIONS OF THE GREEK NEW TESTAMENT
Dates below usually indicate the first edition.

IV. ENGLISH TRANSLATIONS
OF THE NEW TESTAMENT

INDEX OF SUBJECTS